YOUR PARTICULAR GRIEF

BOOKS BY WAYNE E. OATES
Published by The Westminster Press

Your Particular Grief
The Religious Care of the Psychiatric Patient
Pastoral Counseling
When Religion Gets Sick
On Becoming Children of God
Pastoral Counseling in Social Problems:
   Extremism, Race, Sex, Divorce
The Christian Pastor
   (Revised and Enlarged Edition)
Protestant Pastoral Counseling
The Revelation of God in Human Suffering
Anxiety in Christian Experience
The Bible in Pastoral Care

WITH KIRK H. NEELY

   Where to Go for Help
   (Revised and Enlarged Edition)

Christian Care Books
   Books 1-12, edited by Wayne E. Oates

   Pastor's Handbook, Vols. I and II
   by Wayne E. Oates

YOUR PARTICULAR GRIEF

BY

Wayne E. Oates

The Westminster Press
Philadelphia

Scripture quotations from the Revised Standard Version of the Bible are copyrighted 1946, 1952, © 1971, 1973 by the Division of Christian Education of the National Council of the Churches of Christ in the U.S.A., and are used by permission.

BOOK DESIGN BY ALICE DERR

First edition

Published by The Westminster Press®
Philadelphia, Pennsylvania

PRINTED IN THE UNITED STATES OF AMERICA
9 8 7 6 5 4 3 2 1

Library of Congress Cataloging in Publication Data

Oates, Wayne Edward, 1917–
    Your partiular grief.

    1. Consolation.   2. Grief.   I. Title.
BV4905.2.O27   248.8'6   81-3328
ISBN 0-664-24376-2   AACR2

To
Bernard Weisskopf, M.D.

Contents

Preface

THIS BOOK IS THE RESULT OF FORTY YEARS OF CARING FOR BEREAVED persons and of being repeatedly grieved myself. It is intended as a personal communication between you—my reader—and myself. Much technical information underlies its substance. However, no effort is made to belabor you with jargon and the research behind the ideas. That has been done by many others, and myself as well, in other places.

My intention here is to address the uniquely personal grief that you bear. It is almost a letter to those who mourn, with the prayer that you may be comforted in the name and spirit of Jesus Christ.

I am indebted to the faculty of the School of Medicine, especially in the Department of Psychiatry and Behavioral Sciences and at the Child Evaluation Center of the University of Louisville, for their colleagueship in shaping the ideas presented here.

I am especially grateful to Mrs. Jenni Khaliel, my highly competent research assistant, for her invaluable help in gathering information and in preparing the final

manuscript of this book. Her professional skills are a
continuing inspiration and help to me.

W.E.O.

School of Medicine
University of Louisville
Louisville, Kentucky

YOUR PARTICULAR GRIEF

1.

Your Particular Grief

YOU HAVE LOST SOMEONE OR SOMETHING OF GREAT VALUE TO YOU. That loss may have occurred in any one of a number of ways. Grief is often and inevitably caused by death. Grief also is often caused by divorce; by the loss of a particular function of your body such as eyesight, hearing, the ability to talk or walk; or by the loss of a treasured job through resignation or a demand for resignation. Grief is the aftermath of any deeply significant loss.

You grieve differently from other people—not so differently that you cannot find fellowship in suffering with them, yet so differently that no one else's grief is exactly like your own. The loss you have sustained is *your* loss, and your grief is your particular grief.

This book aims to describe at least five kinds of grief that beset people. I hope you will test these descriptions by the kind of suffering you have experienced.

At different times and different places in your spiritual journey you may have experienced more than one—or even all—of these kinds of grief. It is my hope that reading each chapter will enable you to feel understood and at the same time to come to understand better your own particular grief. I also pray that you will be enabled to work through the process of your grieving, and that you will be genuinely comforted by God as you read these pages.

The five kinds of grief I will discuss are as follows. *Anticipatory Grief:* the kind of grief that is a long time coming. *Sudden* or *Traumatic Grief:* the kind of grief that happens with no warning, gives no time for preparation, and strikes like lightning. *No-End Grief:* the kind of grief that seemingly goes on and on, a sort of perpetual sorrow. *Near-Miss Grief:* the kind of grief that comes from having faced the possibility of death or disaster and yet having narrowly escaped such a fate. *Pathological Grief:* the kind of grief that chronically keeps a person from functioning, a disabling sense of distress and impairment of mind and body that calls for medical treatment. In the last chapter, "Grief: A Spiritual Struggle," I have sought to encourage you in the distinctly spiritual struggles of grief and to point toward spiritual recovery from grief.

From this brief outline of the contents of the next six chapters you can see that many factors combine to make each person's grief unique, different from all others. Underlying all of the common types of grief, certain factors make your particular grief distinctly your own.

SHAPERS OF YOUR PARTICULAR GRIEF

Your Unique Relationship

The nature and depth of your relationship to the person whom you have lost is an important variable in how you personally grieve. You may have been related to this person as blood kin but never were deeply involved either positively or negatively. You just have a hard time becoming severely upset the way people are *expected* to be at the loss of a parent, a brother, or a sister. You feel awkward when others *assume* you have many deep, intimate feelings of hurt and loss when you really do not have these at all.

On the other hand, there may be persons with whom you have worked for most of your adult life. You treasure them more than most persons value their blood kin. If something should happen to one of them, you would be devastated.

In another instance, you may have mixed feelings of acceptance and rejection toward the person whom you have lost. If you have lost someone by divorce, this is regularly and readily apparent to you. In fact, one of the heavier parts of the grief is learning what to do about the positive feelings you have toward someone who has rejected you or whom you have rejected by means of a divorce. Or, if you have lost a job that you valued, you may be both relieved and resentful about the circumstances of losing your job. Mixed emotions attend such grief experiences where no death occurred but death wishes abound.

The unique character of your relationship to the person or possession you have lost—its depth or superficiality, its intimacy or coldness, its length or brevity in time—has much to do with the way you mourn.

The Manner of Death or Loss

The circumstances under which a death occurs have much to do with the kind of grief you experience. The suddenness or slowness with which the death of a loved one occurs separates traumatic grief from anticipatory grief. Even so, sudden death by a freak accident, a car crash, or a drowning produces a "cleaner" wound of sorrow than does sudden death by suicide. Even a completed suicide may be the climax of a long, torturous sequence of repeated threats or, in some instances, actual attempts. Still more complicated are those cases where a loved one may have been murdered, especially when the identity of the murderer remains a mystery. Pastoral attention to families in such instances often reveals that the family of the deceased had lived on tenterhooks of dread that something like this would indeed happen. Dignity in death is stolen away from persons who die under humiliating circumstances.

Previous Experience with Grief

You may be a novice at grief; this may be your first encounter with loss. Or you may be a veteran at absorbing losses in your world of relationships. Possibly your many experiences with grief have come in such a short span of time that you did not get over one loss until you were presented with another. One grief has followed upon the other in such rapid succession that you are overwhelmed. Or your many losses may have come at wide enough intervals that the seasoning effect of one helped you to know better how to cope with the next.

However, you may be a new mourner, one who is not acquainted with grief. If so, your grief is thereby qualitatively different from that of the person who is a veteran at grieving. You will need some plain coaching from persons who have been through it themselves. There are organizations such as The Compassionate Friends—a group of volunteers who have joined together as a "life-support system" for persons who have lost a son or daughter in any of the ways that people lose children by death. Your Sunday school class may be a group of persons who study the Bible weekly and who comfort one another in dark times and celebrate with one another on the brighter occasions of life. Furthermore, I hope that you have a pastor to whom you can turn for coaching and caring in your particular grief. Certainly I give thanks that you have begun to read this book and are already being tutored, as it were, in the mystery of human grief.

Grief, you must know, goes through a process in time. You will hear many say "time will heal." Well, time heals, but you need to know *how* it heals. It does so through a series of stages:

1. The stage of *shock* when you get the news.
2. The stage of *numbness* as you try to absorb the shock.
3. The stage of mixed *belief* and *disbelief* that this can really be so.
4. The stage of *depression* and deep mourning when you can sob without control or shame.
5. The stage of *selective memory* when you get along quite well until a fresh reminder of your loss re-presents the whole issue.
6. The stage of *commitment* to start "living again" and rebuilding your life.

These stages take from three to eighteen months, sometimes several years, depending upon a number of variables. Therefore, you should give yourself time to let "grief's slow wisdom" become your own. I have found that just knowing about these six stages has helped many novices at grief to begin learning from their grief to be more patient with life and themselves.

The Timeliness or Untimeliness of the Loss

Losses are namelessly "timed." The Scripture speaks of the days of our years being threescore and ten years, or sometimes—by reason of strength—fourscore. We are admonished to pray: "Teach us to number our days that we may get a heart of wisdom." Intuitively you measure the timeliness or untimeliness of the grief that is uniquely yours. You are more easily prompted to gratitude if your loved one has lived a "full life" and is "ready to go." You can more easily accept this kind of loss. However, if your loved one died an "untimely" death, out of phase and out of cycle, it is likely that a sense of unfairness, even bitterness, will crowd in upon your awareness.

One of the more difficult kinds of grief to bear is that of the person whose loved one does *not* die, but lives a helpless, unconscious, or extremely limited life. The grossly malformed child who has little or no capacity to respond but nevertheless vegetates day in and day out, year in and year out, is one poignant example. Another is the person who has a severe disorder of a type that wipes out cognitive skills, the capacity to communicate, and any ability to care for oneself. Middle-aged persons often suffer severe grief when they are compelled to place their aging parents in a nursing home, especially when meaningful communication with them is practically impossible. If these are examples of your grief, the untimeliness of their not dying causes you to say: "There are many things harder to bear than death."

The Spiritual Resources of the Mourner

You may have come to your experience of grief after a long, depleting series of other events that were fatiguing and stress-ridden. Therefore, the spiritual resources you have with which to face your loss may be in need of replenishment. Or, you may have had smooth sailing thus far. Your strenuous efforts to cope with life have been regularly rewarded with success. You have come to expect not reversal but achievement. Now this! What a rude awakening! Now you can no longer assume everything is going to go your way. Your superficiality has been challenged. You are being pushed into the deeps by the heavy necessity of your loss. What resources of the spirit do you find for coping with these dark griefs?

When you look within for courage and strength to meet this test of your spirit, you realize you have always thought of God as a sort of Santa Claus who simply gives if you are good. Now you are bereft, alone, and desolate. You need a God who is spirit, who is with you, who is your Shield and Defender, who is your Comforter and Deliverer. Yet you are still on another wavelength. You think God is fickle: God has given you your loved one. Now that same God has taken your loved one away. How can you ever forgive God for doing such a thing? But at the core of your being, you really feel—but can't see it to be so—that your loved one has been your god. He or she has left you. You have been abandoned. You have had your foundations shaken. You now begin to realize a kind of spiritual poverty. But be of good cheer, the Lord Jesus Christ perceives a blessedness in your very need. He said: "Blessed are the poor in spirit, for theirs is the kingdom of heaven" (Matt. 5:3). In the depletion of your spiritual resources, you have the beginnings of a new hope: All you need is to feel your need of him.

So the state of your emotional and spiritual resources not only shapes the extent of your grief but it also turns this time of painful trial into a crisis of faith. You are challenged to put away the idolization of your loved one, together with your own expectation that God permits only good things to happen to you. In turn, you discover God as One who suffers with you even as he did with his own Son. You are not alone, for your heavenly Father is with you.

GRIEF IN THE FACE OF LIFE

You may have heard others say about some particular problem: "It is harder to face than death." You may be saying it yourself this very moment because the source of your grief is not the death of a loved one. Rather, you are grieved over something you are having to learn to live with day after day. There is no end to your grief. What are some examples of this "grief in the face of life"?

Probably the most common grief of this nature is the shattering of marriage by *divorce*. The situation is compounded when there are children. Hasty remarriage often tends to ignore the grief that needs time to work through. My own advice to people who have recently been divorced is that they defer considering remarriage until at least one year after the legal decree of the divorce. However, such advice is often hard to implement because marital breakups are often precipitated (not caused) by extramarital commitments to other partners.

Akin to the grief of a divorce is the grief of a *broken courtship*. If this has happened to you, you know that your surrounding friendship group tends to laugh at you. The grief you experience has few community rituals of loving care and concern.

Another grief in the face of life is *retirement*. For some persons retirement is a great deliverance, but for others it is a time of mourning. Your whole life situation changes when you retire, and if you have gotten your main satisfaction in life from your work, then grief is your portion.

Many other griefs in the face of life can be named— severe moral embarrassment, a prison term, the collapse of financial security and/or protracted unemployment, a life-impairing physical handicap, and many more. The main issue is that grief attends many human experiences. With these experiences the next six chapters deal.

2.

Anticipatory Grief

YOU MAY BE INVOLVED AT THIS VERY MOMENT IN CARING FOR A loved one who suffers from an incurable disease such as cancer or leukemia. The severe time-limiting of life by such a disease commits your loved one and you to a long but nevertheless patterned process of grief. We have named this kind of grief "anticipatory grief." By this we mean grief that usually occurs in longer term, incurable diseases and presents sustained and prolonged stress on the patient and his or her family. Nevertheless, this gives time for "prior to death" communication and grief work. The critical issue is: Do the family and the patient, the medical team and the patient, the family and the medical team, actually communicate with each other; or are they isolated from each other, leaving the patient to face death alone? In brief, what kind of communication exists?

RITUALS OF GRIEF

One of the most helpful things I have found in anticipatory grief is to realize that your grief goes through several specific and to-be-expected family and hospital rituals. By "ritual" I mean an accustomed way of doing things, a sort of ceremonial way of dealing with decisions, stresses, and threats, a largely wordless set of actions that are commonly understood and need little explanation. Often these events simply happen; no one plans them. However, as you look back (if your loved one has already died) or as you look around you (if your loved one is now dying), I think my description of these ritual events will become readily apparent to you.

As you read these ritual descriptions, reflect on how you handled or plan to handle each event. Think of how much resentment, fellowship, or straight-on conversation you and your loved one are having or had at the time of these events. If you were to go through these events again, how would you have managed them differently? Or can you lay that question to rest because you did all that could be done? Furthermore, if you are in this process now and your loved one has not yet died, choose a close friend, a relative, a pastor, or a member of the hospital staff such as a physician, nurse, chaplain, or social worker with whom you can "debrief" your feelings as these events occur. Such a person can stimulate good communication between you and your dying loved one. It will also be a healing grace to put your wordless experiences into words as you move through these events.

Similarly, at each of these stages, shape your prayers by asking God for wisdom and patience. The Scripture advises well: "If any of you lacks wisdom, let him ask God, who gives to all . . . generously and without reproaching, and it will be given" (James 1:5). Likewise, let me encourage you to express *all* your feelings to God in prayer, not just the "nice" or "positive" ones. Express any feelings of hurt, frustration, injustice, or even anger in your prayers to God. God can take it! God's love can absorb your bitterest, most painful thoughts and words. The Lord knows us when we sit down and when we stand up, and discerns our thoughts from afar. The Lord searches out our path and our lying down, and is acquainted with all our ways. Even before a word is on our tongues, the Lord knows it altogether (Ps. 139:1-4). Therefore, you can "tell it like it is" to God in prayer and be loved and accepted for your candor, your integrity, and your faithfulness.

We will now look at a number of ritual events in the long process of anticipatory grief.

The Rituals of Urging

At the very outset, your conversation with your loved one began when *you* became concerned about his or her health. You began to *urge* that something be done about it. It may start with *urging* him or her to slow down at work and play, to take some time off to rest, to see what can be done about a vacation. Home remedies of aspirin, diet change, or sleep may be used to stave off symptoms such as pain and general discomfort. For example, a common complaint associated with heart disorder is indigestion.

Yet none of these remedies work. Symptoms persist and intensify. Then you *urge* the loved one to go to a doctor. Interpretation of the symptoms determines *which* doctor to see—a general physician, a cardiologist, etc. You may have to *demand* that a doctor be seen. You may have to go so far as to make the appointment yourself. These are all rituals of urging in which you persuade a loved one to attend to his or her health.

If your loved one is already dead, ask yourself: are you really still "put out" with him or her for not going earlier for diagnosis and treatment? Or do you think you did all that you could? Was it enough to enable you to say: "I did what I thought *at the time* to be right, and I need no longer second-guess myself." Lay all this to rest. Have done with self-accusation. Life has to go on.

The Rituals of Diagnosis

Finally, your loved one has gone to a doctor. Clinical examination is made. Laboratory specimens of blood, urine, fecal matter, etc., are taken. X-rays are taken. Physicians are the "high priests," and technicians are the priestly attendants in these rituals, which are often conducted in the foreign language of "medicalese." Terms like "Pap smear," "BUN," "platelets," are murmured in the examining rooms and the narrow halls. A time of waiting for test results fills you with fear of the unknown. This process includes a longer procedure wherein various tentative hypotheses are ruled out as the cause of the symptoms.

When it is all completed, the final diagnosis of an incurable disease is agreed upon by physicians. Then the critical issue is faced: Shall the patient be told, and if so, how and by whom? Ordinarily, such "telling" is far more than the sharing of known facts. It involves the mental capability of the patient to absorb and compute such knowledge. Extremely aged persons and exceptionally young persons present the hardest dilemmas. Furthermore, patients and families often instinctively enter "protection maneuvers" with each other, i.e., each *knows* the worst, that death is in the offing, but neither wishes to "hurt" the other. The end result is that both are cut off from the support and fellowship they can offer each other. As gently and tenderly as possible, let me suggest that you lay aside this maneuvering. Face the facts together. This does not mean giving up hope, because the battle against these diseases is often won. Rather, it means to join with each other in the battle of treatment. Close ranks. Act on the facts you have. Don't let sentimental notions of "protecting" each other keep you from the strength, wisdom, affection, and healing power God can generate *between* you as you incorporate the diagnosis of an incurable disorder.

If you consider death as a darkness, remember, God is in both the darkness and the light. "Do not go gentle into that good night," as Dylan Thomas says. Rather, look upon it as a mystery to be met with every bit of courage and vigor you are capable of. Nothing can separate you from the love of God—neither life nor death.

The Rituals of Resistance

In your battle with disease you will find yourself at different times attempting to cope in different ways. Elisabeth Kübler-Ross, in her book *On Death and Dying* (Macmillan Co., 1969), describes some of the coping devices you and many others like you are prone to use:

1. *Denial.* Maybe you reject the diagnosis. You refuse to believe that this could possibly happen. You assume that it has happened to others but a miracle will make you an exception. You may think that some exotic cure will make you well again. You—or your loved one, whichever is the stricken patient—will throw yourself into a heavy work schedule to show yourself and others you are well.

2. *Anger.* When denial breaks down, anger may set in. You may lash out at your doctor and say he or she is incompetent. Your irritability may spill over on your closest family members. Both the patient and the family members may be filled with rage. Mobilize this rage to take advantage of every bit of assistance your medical team can provide. Don't let it send you from one doctor to another after you have carefully gotten one or two other medical opinions. Stick with the programs of your

physician and ask for consultation with another physician.

3. *Bargaining.* The seeming magic of the word "if" now becomes a way of coping. *If* the patient does some noble thing, then he or she will be cured. If promises are made to live differently and better, then the patient may assume health will return. Persons with much money may seek to "pay" for a cure.

4. *Depression.* When all measures of bargaining and angers of protest have been exhausted, you and your family may fall into despair. All seems lost. The subtle forces of the act of surrender are taking place. The hard reality of death engulfs the dying person. You can readily see that meeting each other in the depths of despair forms a fellowship of grief. You as a patient grieve doubly—for the failure of your own body to serve well and for the impending separation from loved ones. Your family grieves doubly—for their helplessness to do anything to help and for the loss of their loved one.

Weep with each other at this time. Tell each other how you care and how much you love one another. You may not have done so recently. You may never have done so. Make whatever practical plans need to be made "in the event of death." Put your legal, financial, and personal lives in order. Anyone should have done this already. As usual, few of us keep our affairs in order.

5. *Acceptance.* When you have begun to act upon the reality of imminent death, you enter another phase of surrender and acceptance. A reasonable degree of serenity ensues. Fortunate is the family that can arrive at this acceptance and serenity. In some kinds of disorders, especially heart disorders, serenity is a part of the treatment. The health of the patient may be increased. The patient's way of life now *includes* acceptance of death. In response, the heart itself begins

to function better. Certainly this is the exception and not the usual situation.

These five coping devices have been so widely accepted that you need to examine them closely in the light and darkness of your particular grief. Sometimes these five coping measures are assumed to have a sort of universal *order*, that is, you move from one "stage" to another. Let me caution you *not* to push yourself into an artificial *order* of grief. In one and the same twenty-four-hour period you may feel denial, anger, bargaining, depression, and acceptance. Then again, you may be depressed for a long time and not break out of the depressed state until you can vent your anger, "blow your stack," etc. Then, too, you may be like Robert Browning, a fighter. You may have solved problems all your life by figuratively or actually fighting to the last ditch. Browning said in "Prospice":

I was ever a fighter, so—one fight more,
    The best and the last!
I would hate that death bandaged my eyes, and forebore,
    And bade me creep past.

Similarly, Dylan Thomas adjures his father not to go gently into death, but to rage against it. In other words, *one* of the coping devices mentioned by Kübler-Ross may characterize the *whole* death and dying experience from beginning to end. I have seen mature people simply face the facts of the possibility of death at the outset and live until their death in a mood of undenying acceptance. They, like you, do not fill anybody's time scheme for their death and dying.

Furthermore, Kübler-Ross's schematic does not explicitly refer to observations of some additional coping devices. I would suggest at least the following ones:

1. *Shock.* I often ask patients what they thought about

their diagnosis of incurable illness as soon as they were alone. Many of them tell me that they were overwhelmed and could not think anything. The younger they are, the more likely they are to be shocked. They never dreamed that this could happen to them.

2. *Numbness.* Throughout this book numbness is mentioned repeatedly. I look at this apathy as a sort of God-given anesthetic to protect the whole person as he or she assimilates such shocking news.

3. *Hyperactivity.* Some people react to the news of incurable disorders with a stepped-up level of activity. If time is short, they reason, one had best make every minute count.

4. *Humor.* Little of the copious literature on death and dying mentions the creative use of humor as a way of facing, avoiding, or amending the reality of death. Eugene O'Neill's play *Lazarus Laughed* captures the theme of humor. The gallows humor of military personnel in combat, wounded or not, is a case in point. As a pastor I have seen patients laugh both with tenderness and irony as they planned their funerals in my presence.

5. *Contemplative searching of the meaning of life in the face of death.* Articulate people, disciplined in the use of words, often reflect with friends and loved ones on the meaning of their lives. Others write down—if they are able—what they are thinking and feeling. Either L. D. Johnson's book *The Morning After Death* (Broadman Press, 1978) or C. S. Lewis' book *A Grief Observed* (Bantam Books, 1978) will stimulate this. A careful study of the death, burial, and resurrection narratives in the Gospels and epistles prompts such contemplation and prayer.

6. *The Discipline of Prayer.* In our attempts to control the dying process, we tend to secularize it. Nothing can separate us from the love of God in Jesus Christ, as Paul

says in Romans 8 (vs. 35-39). I recall, as a young chaplain, visiting a revered teacher during his last illness. He asked me to kneel by his bed that he might give me his blessing by praying for both of us. In his prayer, he gave thanks for his life and for his hope for the gift of a new life in the resurrection. He made a general confession of sin for both of us. Then he prayed that the mantle of the prophets and the apostles would be borne by me with strength, discipline, and courage. After his prayer, he conversed with me about how important the care of the sick is when done in Christ's name. Time would fail me to describe all such evidences of companionship with God in facing death that I have been privileged to share.

In no wise am I being super pious to insist on this dimension of coping with a fatal diagnosis and resisting death's too-early arrival. Rather, I am forthrightly seeking to make the clinical record accurate.

The Rituals of the Family Gathering and Leave-Taking

As the time of death approaches and before the patient loses consciousness, relatives who are present have an accustomed way of calling those who live at a distance. They say: "If you want to talk with her (or him) you had better come quickly." Then the family begins to gather. This gathering of the clan may bring more strain to you. If you and relatives who live at a distance are not on good terms, or if you simply do not see each other often, tension increases.

In any event, it is important that you and they say those loving things that you have always thought but never said to the patient. If you cannot get to the patient at this time, write a letter expressing all the things for which you are grateful. Express the genuine feelings of love and respect you hold for the patient. I have seen people do this when the patient could not hear well and yet could read. The results have been greatly helpful. This will do you and the patient much good. Much healing and reconciliation can take place if you do these things at this time.

The Rituals of Prolongation of Life

At this time of extremity it will be necessary to decide how much artificial maintenance of life you deem wise, humane, and necessary. Feeding by intravenous tubes, giving oxygen by nasal tubes, sustaining heart action by artificial means, draining urine by catheter, are a few of the extraordinary means for sustaining biological functions long after conscious awareness is gone. If the patient remains at home, then the question of whether to use extraordinary measures does not have to be decided. Hence, many people today *ask* to be allowed to die at home where death is natural and where there are no "No Visitors" signs. Grandchildren or children can move in and out in their own unique ways of caring for a dying person. Personally, I prefer it this way. However, many people today do not have a home where this is possible. Members of families have jobs to maintain. Nursing assistance is both expensive and hard to find. As a result, hospitals are the place where many people die. Yet if the home can be a place of dying, I think it should be considered.

In a hospital, however, the decisions as to how often a patient should be resuscitated after cardiac arrest, or how much equipment should be used to maintain a state of vegetation, are usually made by a quiet consensus. Family, physicians, and nurses tend to arrive at a common understanding without conflict. Television shows and news media do not leave this impression.

The Rituals of the Vigil at the Death Itself

The need to be beside a dying person at the moment of death to stand vigil seems to be universal. One woman told me that the reason she wanted to be present was to ask of God in prayer a few more years to be with her husband. On the first occasion he did come back from the edge of life, and lived three more years. During the next vigil he died. Some say that they keep vigil so they can comfort each other in time of trial.

Standing vigil is a great tradition in Catholicism. It is particularly a time when prayers may be sung or said in behalf of the dying. No church requirement is made of pastors and chaplains among Protestants. Nevertheless, when a pastor or chaplain actually stands vigil with the family, it seems that a lasting bond of affection in suffering is formed. Let me suggest, therefore, that you call your chaplain, priest, rabbi, or pastor at such a time as this.

The Rituals of Notification

If you have never experienced the loss of a loved one by death, you may wonder what to do when it happens. Many people have to be notified. The attending physician is usually notified by the nurses. Upon the physician's having pronounced the patient dead and having signed a death certificate, the nurse then often calls the funeral director/mortician for you. You will need to have decided whom to call upon. Also, you will need the deceased's social security number. This amounts to surety for the basic expenses of burial. Provide these two pieces of information for the nurse's call. If the patient dies at home, then members of the family, your pastor, or the physician can make these calls.

The notification of relatives both near and far becomes necessary. Some of them you yourself will want to call.

Beyond a certain point, however, calling relatives and friends can best be done by a friend. Often this friend is your pastor or a chaplain. Such a person has ordinarily had both training and experience and knows how to do this well.

The Rituals of Funeral Planning and the Funeral Itself

The discipline of outlining with your pastor, priest, or rabbi just what you want the funeral to be like is an important part of the grief work in which you are now engulfed. The kinds of Scripture, prayers, and music that you have learned were important to the deceased will be good information for the minister to use. Family members will often lean over backward to include many pastors lest one get his or her feelings hurt. *Don't do it.* I have been a minister for over forty years. I have seen pastors get their feelings hurt over many things. I have never seen or heard of one being hurt by not being included in a funeral ceremony. We are without exception committed to your comfort, not our own, at such a time as this.

The funeral itself has several purposes. You will be strengthened more to have these in mind. The purposes of the funeral are:

1. To gather the people of God around you to assure you that you are not alone as you take your grief to God in prayer.
2. To direct all your and your family's grief to God in worship. God is eternal and we are mortal. God is the God who overcomes death by granting to us a resurrected body in Jesus Christ. Christian worship helps you look death in the face and not run away. God in Christ enables you to stand and, having stood all, to stand nevertheless.

3. To enable you and your fellow mourners to commemorate all that is eternal in the life and work of your loved one. The funeral gives friends a chance to say to you how valuable your loved one has been to their lives.
4. To clinch in your mind that indeed and in fact your loved one is dead. This is the beginning of your recovery from grief.

The Rituals of the Division of Property

You would think that you have been through enough. You are still exhausted from caring for your loved one in the long illness, from the vigil, and from the funeral itself. Before you can catch your breath you meet questions about what to do with his or her "things." Things have symbolic power far beyond their cash value. You are well advised not to make quick and hurried decisions about your living arrangements, such as selling your home or "breaking up housekeeping." Stay put and delay making that large decision for six months to a year, if indeed you ever make it.

However, your immediate decisions will be about personal effects: clothes, jewelry, tools, books, written materials including correspondence. My suggestion is that you ask the most widely accepted and trusted survivor to help you make these decisions. Ask who wants what and make decisions about these things as soon as possible. Then you won't feel that "heavy, heavy hangs over your head" each time you see these things.

Accomplishing this task is another long step forward in your grieving process. You see, you can follow these rituals and have some guideposts to your progress through your grief.

The Rituals of Revisiting the Grave

The burial site, or the location of the ashes in the case of cremation, is a place of unusual importance to you now. You will, if you have not already done so, find yourself wanting to visit this place. Doing so will help you to get through mourning. Take a trusted relative, friend, or church member with you. This gives you a living person with whom to put into words how you are feeling. As time moves forward, you should feel less and less inclined to make these journeys. For the first year after the death, you will tend to visit the grave more often. Then you will tend to go only when relatives who live at a distance return. Then you and they make a sort of pilgrimage together.

Whatever you do, do not make a shrine of the burial place. Keep yourself from idolizing the deceased. Recognize that there is a persistent temptation to replace God with a human substitute.

The Rituals of the Thinning of the Crowd

Immediately after a death, crowds of people come expressing their condolences to you. A few weeks pass by. This crowd thins out. A very few intimate "old standbys" stay with you. By now you have resumed your routine, even though your routine has to be overhauled. You no longer gear your whole life to the needs of a fatally ill person. You have—if you are holding down a job—returned to work. The routine itself stabilizes your feelings and keeps you on track. Weekends, vacations, and free time hang heavily on your hands.

Three great holiday seasons mark times of family gatherings from which the deceased is absent. Thanksgiving, Christmas, and Easter seem unusually heavy and difficult times for you. Let me suggest that at the main mealtime on these occasions you have someone read Scripture, offer prayer, and give thanks for the life of the deceased and the fellowship of those present. If you feel up to it, do this yourself. On Thanksgiving, good Scriptures to read are Isa. 40:28-31 and Ps. 103:1-5. On Christmas, read Isa. 40:1-11 and Matt. 2:1-6. On Easter, you will find John 11:17-27 and I Cor. 15:51-58 useful. Compose a brief time of worship. Ask God's encouragement in the brave rebuilding of life in which you are engaged. Take this text as your guiding commitment:

> Not that I have already obtained this or am already perfect; but I press on to make it my own, because Christ Jesus has made me his own. Brethren, I do not consider that I have made it my own; but one thing I do, forgetting what lies behind and straining forward to what lies ahead, I press on toward the goal for the prize of the upward call of God in Christ Jesus. (Phil. 3:12-14)

The first anniversary of the death of your loved one holds special significance, also. Do not be surprised if you are more pensive and somewhat nostalgic and depressed on this day. Make plans to "play taps" for your grief at this time. I learned this figure of speech in conversing with an Army widow. She and a beloved daughter went to the deceased father's grave. They stood together and held hands as they silently remembered the playing of taps. They dedicated themselves to having done with grief. The American people need an additional ritual that does indeed call into a fellowship persons who will share in the commitment to have done with grief.

For many years after the death of Peter Marshall, his widow, Catherine, wrote books that enshrined her husband in the hearts of millions. After a while she decided that it was time to have done with grief and to get on with life without Peter Marshall. She wrote a book entitled *To Live Again* (1957; Avon Books, 1972). In it she told of the ways in which she was having done with grief.

God "has made everything beautiful in its time; also he has put eternity into man's mind," says Eccl. 3:11. There is "a time to weep, and a time to laugh." The time to weep is past—especially weeping for ourselves. The time to laugh is at hand when, with a friend who knew the deceased, you can join in free and easy laughter at some amusing incident you, your friend, and your deceased loved one shared together. Then you are ready to live again.

PREVENTIVE SPIRITUAL HEALTH MEASURES
IN ANTICIPATORY GRIEF

You want to ensure that the rest of your life, in spite of your loss, is lived to the outer limits of health, creative usefulness, and personal happiness. Let me suggest some ways of doing so.

First, do not feel guilty about feeling relieved of the stresses of daily caring for your deceased loved one. Those days were filled with stress and the fear of the unknown. Now you have whole sections of a day left vacant by the death of your loved one. You may rebuke yourself for the sense of relief from stress. You no longer struggle with the unknown. You know that death has come. It has a cold sense of finality about it. However, you know what you are dealing with.

Caring for this person and doing all that you knew how to do gave you a real feeling of being needed. In the relief from the struggle, you may enjoy—for a time—feeling free of such heavy responsibility. You have a right to that enjoyment. Thank God for it and take heart.

Second, find a new place in life. Your fatally ill loved

one—in his or her dying days—without effort gave you a "place" in life. You knew your place and fulfilled its demands with valor and consistency. In a sense this was a "place in the sun" as well as a "place in the dark." People knew you, responded to you, and revered you for the place you served. Now you no longer have that place. It is empty. Three months pass and the crowd thins out and leaves you without that particular place in their lives. In his fine book entitled *A Place for You* (Harper & Row, 1968), Paul Tournier says that life itself moves on a reliable principle of "leaving a place and seeking and finding another place." He says that faith in God means to accept this principle, to leave the old place, and to seek a new one. As The Letter to the Hebrews states it: "For here we have no lasting city, but we seek the city which is to come" (Heb. 13:14). The substance of faith is to seek that new place God has for you, even though you cannot seek it now. "Faith is the assurance of things hoped for, the conviction of things not seen" (Heb. 11:1). You have been through an ordeal of suffering. That suffering is equipping you for a new place in life. Do not let the nostalgia and sentimentality and self-pity keep you from finding that new place. You have not been called to the past, to self-pity, or to weeping for yourself. You have been called to seek a new place of creative caring for other people.

Third, assess your relationship to those loved ones who are still living. For example, the loss of a youthful son or daughter in youth, out of time, out of cycle, out of season, is one of the bitterest losses to swallow. You may be so caught up in your bitterness about losing this one son or daughter that you cannot prize, treasure, and enjoy all the more the sons and daughters who are alive, well, and present with you. After a reasonable period of mourning, you will wear these living sons and daughters down to impatience, a feeling of rejection, and avoidance if you continue to be obsessed with the loss of their brother or sister. Your interest in *their* feelings will keep your own sense of what is important in balance. Reserve the continuing pain of your loss for people your own age and for conferences with your pastor.

Similarly if your husband or wife died, you may hang on to one of your sons or daughters to the point that his or her marriage is dominated by the incessant demands you make for time and attention. You *control* this son or daughter by means of your grief. Thus your grief ceases to be a suffering from which to recover; it becomes a tool with which to stay in the center of a son's or daughter's (usually a daughter's) attention. Your grief becomes a test of affection. That is, if this child loves you, he or she will respond to your every twinge of unhappiness. Without intending to do so, you have actually become a cruel taskmaster. Have done with such a way of life.

Fourth, replenish your friendship group with persons your own age. These persons are part of your life-support system and you are part of theirs. Think of this: How many new people have you met and come to know in the last six months? A great part of finding a new place in life and avoiding a demanding relationship to relatives begins by replenishing your friendships with old friends with whom you have lost contact and with new friends you have not known before. This is one of God's favorite ways of "making all things new" for you. Your church is a natural place for this to happen.

To make and maintain new friends, you must avoid becoming a bore by constantly rehearsing your grief to them. At the beginning of your relationship, it may be well and good for you to convey to them just how you hurt. When an anniversary of the death of your loved one comes, it is important to "debrief" your feelings with your friends. They will want to share their hurts with you, too. However, if *every* contact with them is devoted to *wailing*, you will soon find that they are too busy with other things. Your constant wailing has made a bore of you. You complain of loneliness, but you assure that you will continue to be lonely by being boresome. Boring people tend to be lonely people. Interesting people tend to have friends to spare. You are no exception to this simple maxim. You are not called to be a bore. God has a better way of life for you.

Fifth, reassess your *inner* resources in contemplation of God. God made not only your loved one but you and me to be limited in our length of days. Death is a part of creation. Life would be unbearable without it. There are kinds of grief and events that cause grief that will make you realize that many things are worse than death. In all these things, however, we are more than conquerors through the Lord Jesus Christ, who loved us and gave himself for us.

Therefore, search out the power that is within you. In what way have you placed your dead loved one at the center of your life, thereby displacing God's sovereignty at the center of your devotions? No one can understand, accept, love, and forgive you for this idolatry half as much as God can. God gave his own Son in death that you and I might grasp and be grasped by the power of his resurrection. This God is a God of the living, not of the dead. This God beckons you to a "re-centering" of life around fellowship with him, his Son, and the gift of the Spirit through the resurrection.

Therefore, find a new companionship with God in your meditations. Contemplate the presence of God as you spend some of your lonely times in thinking and reading. You may feel angry at God, as I have indicated before. Read Psalm 22. You may feel the silence of God.

Read Psalm 28. You may find the thoughts of C. S. Lewis helpful. He says of his own grief upon the loss of his wife: "It is hard to have patience with people who say, 'There is no death,' or 'Death doesn't matter.' There is death and whatever is matters, and whatever happens has consequences. . . . She died. She is dead. Is the word so difficult to learn? . . But her voice is still vivid. The remembered voice—that can turn me into a whimpering child . . . . Am I . . . just sidling back to God because I know if there's any road to H. [Lewis' wife], it runs through Him? But then of course I know perfectly well that He can't be used as a road. If you are approaching Him not as the goal but as a road, not as an end, but as a means, you're really not approaching Him at all." (*A Grief Observed*, pp. 16, 79.)

Recentering your life is a major spiritual challenge. May God redeem both you and me from idolatry of our own flesh-and-blood loves. When that truly happens we will stay well indeed.

Finally, praying that you are "on your own before God," let me join with you as we both take our burdens of guilt to God and leave them with God. You may feel some sense of guilt or shame in relation to your deceased loved one. Ordinarily this guilt arises out of your own expectations of yourself—that you *should* have done this, that, or the other thing. If *only* you had done something other than what you did, he or she would not have died. In fact you are mourning your own limited strength, a thing you share with all of us.

Or it may be that some real act was done for which you feel guilty. Bring it out into the open in your prayers and ask God's forgiveness. Then ask God for the strength to forgive yourself for your act and for the sin of having made your conscience your god instead of the God and Father of our Lord Jesus Christ, the Father of mercies and the God of all comfort. Accept the freedom from guilt that God gives you. Have done with self-blame and get on with life.

If you cannot experience this freedom from guilt at this point, probe more deeply. It could be that you do not think God can forgive you because some other person has done something to you which you cannot forgive. It may have been some neglect of the deceased by someone just as responsible as you were. It may be that someone has used legal maneuvers to carry away the lion's share of the inheritance money and property. It may be that you have been stuck with paying all the medical and funeral bills and no one else in the family will turn a hand to help you. You might, in another instance, notably have nursed one parent through a final illness, but now you have the continuing care of the other parent. You may have been close to the deceased parent and at total odds with the remaining one. You may feel guilty for the fleeting thought: "Why was it *this* one who died and *not* the other?"

Being forgiven by God means setting straight your situation by confronting the offending one if need be and doing so in a spirit of gentleness, looking to yourself lest you also be tempted. Read Gal. 6:1-5 and Matt. 18:15-20. The Lord's Prayer, Matt. 6:9-14, is another passage to read. God's intention is that through love every barrier will be broken down and every guilt will be lifted. Your destiny is freedom from guilt. Do not let the yoke of some unforgiven friend or relative steal away your freedom. Christ set you free. Take heed that these old feelings do not entangle you in bondage.

3.
Sudden or Traumatic Grief

YOUR PARTICULAR GRIEF MAY WELL NOT FIT THE PICTURE I HAVE given of anticipatory grief. The reason is simple: Death came to your loved one all of a sudden, like a bolt of lightning "out of the blue." There was no time for anticipation. Therefore, I want to discuss sudden or traumatic grief in this chapter. This may be more precisely where you are in your life.

FACTORS IN TRAUMATIC GRIEF

Traumatic grief is sudden in its onset. It comes with little or no previous warning and is loaded with surprises. This kind of grief has its own unique features. Let us see whether your experience has these marks of sudden or traumatic grief.

Shock

The first feature of sudden grief is shock. Death, or any other life-changing event—such as divorce, or the sudden loss of a job one has assumed would last a lifetime—always comes with a certain amount of shock. Anticipatory grief never does away with the shock that comes with the event itself. However, sudden grief has an intensity far beyond that of anticipatory grief.

Shock has an impact upon your physical body. In medical terms, you need to be aware of the sudden disturbance of your very body. There is an acute peripheral circulatory failure caused by the derangement of your circulatory control or a loss of circulating fluid. Shock is marked by a lowering of blood pressure, coldness of skin, rapid heartbeat, and an acute sense of terror. Therefore, you may remember some severe and strange physical symptoms upon having learned of the sudden loss of your loved one. You may have needed medical attention at the time, and this is good. You will know by this that if such a thing ever happens to you or to anyone close to you, a physician should be given an emergency call. Those of us who work in emergency rooms in large hospitals know that shock can disable or even kill a person who has just seen a spouse shot by armed robbers or killed in an accident. Therefore, preventive health care calls for the presence of a physician at such a time as this. As a pastor, I routinely see to it that a physician is called when I am called to sudden death scenes.

You may have already weathered the shock of sudden grief. Yet you still have physical symptoms. Let me urge you to make an appointment to see your physician. A large part of successfully enduring this grief is staying well. Your physician can help you to do so. If you have any trouble sleeping, eating or digesting your food, or breathing, or have noticed strange activity of your heart, your physician can advise you and treat these trouble signs in your physical health.

Shock is also a psychological event of much significance. Some psychological features of shock may help you to sort out your own thought processes and feeling responses to sudden grief:

1. *Alarm.* Your whole outlook on life and the routine of your day are thrown into alarm. A fire alarm was sounded in the building where I work. All delicately balanced schedules were interrupted. At first most of the staff said: "Oh, it's nothing; just a practice drill." But indeed there was a fire in one of the laboratories. The full force of the city's firefighters, equipment and all, was soon brought into action. Shocking news of a sudden loss brings all your mental and emotional resources into action, too. In the twinkling of an eye everything is changed and thrown into disarray. Your emergency alarm system goes off. You are in a state of alarm.

2. *Disbelief.* A second feature of shock is disbelief. You simply cannot believe your own eyes and ears. You may challenge the newsbearer to prove what has been reported. The characteristic response, "Oh, no!" best describes this aspect of shock. All of the meaningful linkups of your life are in jeopardy. To keep the world sane and sensible, this harsh news just *cannot* be so.

3. *Panic.* The terror of realizing that sudden news *is* true panics you. You may lose control completely and say and do things that in your ordinary composure you would never say or do. The shock of the news you have received throws everything into pandemonium and you panic.

Shock, then, is made up of alarm, disbelief, and panic, to say the least. If you look back on your reactions upon hearing of the sudden death of a loved one, you will likely see those things in yourself. One value of describing them is to tell you that you are not alone; others have these strange experiences also. Blessed are you if you have come through this phase of your grief and have a company of understanding friends around you. If you are still isolated and alone with these feelings, reach out to a friend, a pastor, a physician, and "debrief" by sharing your memories. This will help assure that alarm, disbelief, and panic will not have a continuing power over you.

Numbing

A second result of sudden grief is numbing. I learned this word from persons who, after learning of a sudden loss, said: "I feel numb all over." "Dazed" is another word for it. This numbing is a sort of natural anesthetic that keeps you from experiencing the total pain of your loss all at once. You have been dealt a blow for which you—and your whole organism—were unprepared. In God's amazing providence, you are given a "protective shield." Robert Jay Lifton quotes the words of a person who, like you, had been hit by a sudden grief:

> The whole situation around me was very special. . . . About life and death . . . I just couldn't have any reaction. . . . I don't think I felt any joy or sadness. . . . My feelings about death weren't really normal. . . . You might say I became insensitive to death. (*The Broken Connection,* p. 174; Simon & Schuster, 1979)

In this time of "insensitivity" you may be pulled along by the details of a day's work. You prepare breakfast as usual. You do all the things required of you by mechanical routine. You move through events in a daze. Your routine of life is a great strength to you at this time. One young mother, whose husband had been shot down in aerial combat, told me: "Everything within me just shut down when I learned that. What kept me going was the baby's cries for my help. She just kept me at living."

The Recovery and Identification of the Body

Another unique factor in traumatic grief is the recovery and identification of the body. Some examples make clear how important this is. A young businesswoman in my city disappeared. Her body was found in a car in many feet of water in the river. The process of recovering the body was a grief in its own right. The exact cause for her death was still a mystery two weeks after the recovery of the body. The identification of the body for members of the family was a wrenching, gruesome procedure, the memories of which multiply the strength of grief concerning her death. Another example is the recovery and identification of the bodies of the more than nine hundred bodies in the Jonestown mass suicide. Many families of these persons may never know *whether* their loved one was in the group or not. A less publicized example is that of the twenty-year-old young man killed in a plane accident. His mother had recently been divorced from his father. Now this! Yet, she had the ghastly responsibility of positively identifying his body. The memories of these events make one's recovery from grief more difficult.

One of the most traumatic kinds of grief is the suicide of someone close to you. The recovery of the body is often difficult, especially if the person accomplished suicide by drowning or by inflicting a fatal shotgun wound. The recovery of a suicide note often has highly complicating effects on the grief of the survivors. The blaming force of such a note may be lasting in its effects. If this has happened to you, remember one thing: The initial and final responsibility for a suicide is upon the person who did it, not upon you or anyone else. Grieve because of the loss of the person, but do not accept responsibility or feel guilty for an act that was not yours and over which you had no final control.

A disclaimer needs to be entered here. Not all suicides are sudden and unanticipated. In some instances the person has repeatedly threatened to commit suicide. By this means a long, torturous, despotic power is exerted over others. In such instances, the suicide actually completed amounts to the final scene of a long anticipated and feared death.

The recovery of the body and exact identification is an acute issue in catastrophic death. As I write these words, thousands of people have been buried beneath mountains of debris in an earthquake zone in Italy. Not too long ago Mt. St. Helens erupted and many people are missing and assumed to be dead. That assumption is easy for rescue workers, but catastrophic for a member of the person's family.

The most devastating catastrophe is war. Earthquakes, volcanic eruptions, hurricanes, fires, and floods are felt to be beyond human control. War, however, is perpetrated by men. I use the word "men" here purposely, because as of now war is a unique way *men* have of presumably "solving" national and international problems. Having lived through four wars, I am more impressed with the incalculable problems war creates than with the vague problems it is assumed to have solved. The seeds of other wars are sown in the treaties that "end" wars.

War's catastrophic effects are individually felt when members of families are wounded in action, missing in action, or killed in action (WIA, MIA, or KIA).

In all these catastrophes, the recovery and identification of the body is critical in your recovery from grief. Is the body they found *really* my loved one or is it someone else? Sealed caskets are common in such deaths. "Seeing for yourself" is a needed part of your closure, your recognition that death has really occurred. Without this, you are prone to fantasize that someday he or she will come walking back into your life. Your anger at the clumsiness of the rescue workers, the government, the police, or the military further confirms your helpless denial of the reality of death. This is intensified in the "no end in sight" grief in those instances where no body was found.

Living life to the fullest day by day in spite of this uncertainty is a spiritual discipline for survival. Life thrives on finishing one thing and starting another. But mysteriously, some griefs are never completed, as we shall see in discussing no-end grief in Chapter 4 of this book.

Delayed Grief Work

The shock and the numbing serve to delay your recovery from sudden and traumatic grief. The events of the funeral, the division of the property, the thinning of the crowd, and the return to the normal routines of life are likely to move too rapidly. You are left to your own spiritual resources all too soon. A lot of inner turmoil is to be faced without the accustomed life support of your friendship groups, your church family, or your work groups of colleagues and fellow workers.

One important principle must guide your thinking and acting about yourself in sudden grief: *Your grief work will be longer, lonelier, and more hazardous to your lasting emotional stability than if you had been able to anticipate the loss and to converse with your loved one before death.* Take a look at each of these assertions.

The length of grief work is extended. Do not use the commonly accepted "one year" rule for having done with grief. Give yourself more time than this. For example, do not make quick decisions about other life-changing issues. Do not quickly change your place of residence and thereby disrupt your friendship group after having lost your loved one. A grown person's life is like a tree; you don't uproot it as readily as you would if it were much younger. Do not add shock to shock. You have enough as it is.

Also, if you have lost a spouse, do not hurry into another marriage. You will be prone to try to "replace" the deceased spouse rather than to work through grief and to form a new relationship in a natural and leisurely way.

Further, do not quickly give up your work or change jobs unless external necessity forces it upon you. The routine of your work and the camaraderie of your associates serve as strong supports as your feelings of numbness wear off and the pain of the loss is more clearly felt.

Put all of these big, life-changing decisions "on hold" for at least a year or eighteen months. Bear in mind that *a sudden grief simply takes more time for recovery than other kinds of grief.* Do not hurry or push yourself unduly. Other stresses over which you do have control should be spread over a longer span of time.

Again, *your sudden grief has to be borne more by yourself than do other kinds of grief.* The circumstances of the death cause this loneliness. The members of the family whose daughter was mysteriously drowned are in a class by themselves in their grief. Not many can say: "Something very similar, if not the same, happened to me." No, they are practically unique. Uniqueness isolates them. In another instance the family of a young man who was killed or remains missing in action in Vietnam is also an exceptional case. A small portion of the population are enduring a disproportionate share of the grief in that war. Because few people can identify with them their loneliness is greater.

Therefore, persons suffering traumatic grief have a greater need for fellowship with other people. They are lonelier in their grief. I have the privilege of knowing a bright and creative young man whose mother entered a mental hospital when he was less than a year old. Then his father abandoned him. When he was seventeen his mother died, having been in a state mental hospital all the life of this young man. At eighteen he was drafted into the Army and sent to Vietnam. He returned safely. When I first met him, he was filled with grief and rage. For the first time he found in me and my students a group of people who would get under the load of grief with him and start the process of recovery. Up until we met him, he had borne it all alone. We met him when he was thirty-one years old.

Whatever else you do, by all means reach out and select a meaningful fellowship with a caring community. You may be disappointed several times, but keep at it until you find and form a fellowship of two, three, four, or more people who sustain you in your grief and whom you can sustain in their grief. You become special to them and they become special to you.

The hazards to your basic emotional stability. Sudden grief can be bizarre and demonic enough to threaten to unhinge your emotional stability. Everything that can be shaken is being shaken by the untoward circumstances of your loss. Therefore, take steps to ensure your emotional stability now and in the future. You can ensure your health and well-being by doing some specific things in addition to what I have already suggested.

First, confer with your family physician about your own physical health and the health of each member of your family. Ask for any available wisdom of a preventive as well as a therapeutic nature. If you are a woman, confer with your gynecologist, who may be of more specific help to you as a woman.

Second, search your community for a competent counselor. This may be your parish minister, who often has more specific training in grief therapy than almost any other profession. It may be a pastoral counselor in a counseling service near you. The chaplain in a local hospital can help you find these counseling centers. It may be a mature and wise psychiatrist. In the event that you lost your loved one by suicide or by some extremely bizarre cause, this psychiatrist usually has had the kind of training to orient you to the strange realities with which you are having to deal. Do not let the usual stigma about consulting a psychiatrist hinder you from using a valuable ally in keeping your own equilibrium. A psychiatrist is no stranger to the kind of situation you will describe. If you are having trouble locating a psychiatrist, ask your pastor, your comprehensive mental health center, the administrator of your local hospital, or the local city or county medical society, who can recommend names to you.

The children and adolescents who are related to the deceased are in a highly vulnerable condition. Separately and as a group they need professional attention that does not "tag" or "label" them as unusual. Your church is a strong source of such help. Pastors, youth ministers, ministers of music, and ministers of education often have ready and easy access to these children. Such persons should be considered and enlisted as personal counselors to them. Also, a Family Service agency near you will have staff members who are well trained to provide service to you and the whole family.

I emphasize these measures because I work in a large

medical center in a department of psychiatry and a
department of pediatrics. We see many people who are
reeling under the blow of sudden death or other kinds of
tragedy. We assume that a person who has been hit by
grief in a sudden way is more vulnerable to emotional
illness later on. Therefore, I am interested in *preventing*
this from happening by suggesting that you get
professional assistance *before* such complications arise.

Areas of Vulnerability

If what I have just said is so, you have the right to ask:
"What *are* some of the areas in which a person who
experiences sudden grief is more vulnerable to later
emotional illness?" Let me describe several factors in
sudden grief that predispose a person to emotional
problems. Also, I can suggest several ways to prevent
such problems.

First, sudden grief delays the grief work because of
shock and numbing until long past the time that relatives
and friends have thinned out and gone about other
concerns. At the end of three, six, or nine months the
shock and numbness wear off. Then as a bereaved person
you tend to experience the tears, the depression, the
fantasy, and the agony of your loss. Then you are much
more likely to be alone with your grief. Furthermore, you
are more likely to *interpret* these heavy emotions as mental
instability on your part. If you could just straighten up
and fly right, you may say to yourself, these feelings
would go away. You are less likely to let yourself go and
cry, grieve, and ask for an understanding ear.

If this is the case with you, you can find understanding
with someone else in your community who has been
through a similar traumatic grief. Also, your pastor or
one of the counselors on the staff of a pastoral counseling

center has ordinarily been trained to help you at this time. Yours is a common experience that experienced counselors often see. Whatever you do, *do not let yourself get isolated by these feelings; share them with trusted people.* The element of isolation is an outstanding feature of persons who have broken down in distress and have to be hospitalized. This need not happen if you begin early to reach out to the "significant others" in your life.

Second, sudden grief often leads to emotional imbalance because the circumstances of the loss seem more unjust and unfair. Sudden grief is out of phase as to when loss is ordinarily expected. Because of real injustice and unfairness, you are tempted by the fantasy that in your own strength you can set everything right, get even, and retaliate against those whom you consider to be the agents of the injustice. Therefore, you organize your whole family, your work, your religion, and everything else around the vendetta of vengeance. This becomes an obsession, a cry for sympathy, and an attempt to rewrite history.

You can prevent this from happening if you sit down with a trusted friend, pastor, or physician and "face up" to your own spirit of revenge. All your heroics are not going to right the great injustice: They won't bring the dead to life again. Ask a trusted person for some time, and plan to talk about nothing else. When you get to the bottom of it, you may confess that you have appointed yourself judge, jury, and executioner. You are taking vengeance out of God's hands and playing god yourself. This is too much for anyone to attempt. You do so only at the peril of your own sanity. Life is too short for that. I have a close and dear friend who is a devout Roman Catholic. When faced with a totally frustrating situation, he says that he "offers it up." He offers it up to God to let God work it out while he gets on with things that are hurting to be done which God has placed in his hands to do.

So, can you offer up this grief and start putting things in perspective? I hope so. It is urgent that you do so.

Third, sudden grief, in some instances, leads to emotional imbalance because some people tend to try to solve all problems by more and more activity. In one instance I saw a widow start a degree program in a university, take on a series of heavy responsibilities within her church, and accept a full-time job within three weeks of the tragic death of her husband by suicide. Such frenetic activity prevents a person from taking time for conversation with a friend, a pastor, a physician, or an understanding and loving relative. She sought to "seal over" the severe wound she had sustained. Finally, friends confronted her with this in a firm but gentle way. She slowed down, unloaded some of the extraneous duties, and listened carefully to her children's needs. She found a sustaining counselor and a group with whom she could face her deepest feelings of rejection, anger, and hurt brought on by her husband's suicide. Hyperactivity, if kept up, would have exhausted her until finally her health would fail. Somehow she learned that she did not have to get sick to deserve the attention, care, and affection of others. Being sick is a terrible price to pay for what a community of grace is ready to give freely.

Fourth, another reason why sudden death and traumatic grief resulting from it may lead to emotional disorder is that the mourner is left *helpless* in a strange way. In anticipatory grief, one may have done all that could be done, even more than could be rightly expected. By the time of the death, the mourner is exhausted from doing. Death even brings a sense of relief. However, sudden death leaves no opportunity to prepare for loss. One simply stands there helpless, all chance of doing anything snatched away. Consequently, the sense of helplessness can continue to overwhelm until a person cannot function.

At the root of this sense of helplessness is the deeper desire always to be in control. Persons who are managers, controllers, and doers in life are accustomed to "calling the shots." They determine the course of things. Yet here is a major life situation in which such a person is as helpless as a newborn baby. There is *nothing* he or she can do. Some people can face up to their helplessness, admit their style of controlling everything, and even laugh mirthlessly and ironically about it. Other persons refuse to face it. They are angered if this human foible is pointed out to them, and their own life tends to go out of control. Such persons may become severely depressed, filled with self-directed rage at not having been in control of their deceased loved one's total destiny.

Do these thumbnail sketches touch any familiar chords in your life? You *can* do something about your own perspective and response to the harsh fact of your loss. You can *accept* your own finite limitations and lack of control over all the factors that led up to the death of your loved one. You may not be able to do even this in your own strength. That is how helpless most of us are most of the time. Yet, with the encouragement of a friend, a pastor, a teacher, or a physician, or a wonderful combination of all of them, you can "admit that you are powerless over your grief, and that your life is becoming unmanageable." You can believe that there is a Power greater than yourself who can restore your life to the sanity you deserve.

The hard shock and heavy numbness can wear off and you can begin to recover from your loss. As one gospel song puts it:

Down in the human heart, crushed by the tempter,
   Feelings lie buried that grace can restore;
Touched by a loving heart, wakened by kindness,
   Chords that are broken will vibrate once more.

SOME GUIDES TO SPIRITUAL HEALTH
IN THE FACE OF SUDDEN GRIEF

If persons who are struck by sudden grief are more at risk for a pathological kind of grief, what steps can be taken to prevent this from happening?

Sudden Death: Heart Failure

If your loved one died of a heart attack with no previous warning, then you can ward off pathological complications by doing several practical things. First, be sure that an autopsy is done. The laboratory findings take some of the mystery out of the cause of death. Second, see a heart specialist yourself and get a professional estimate of your own cardiovascular condition. This realistically forestalls fears you may develop that the same thing will happen to you. Third, if your deceased relative had any habits that contributed to heart disorder—such as smoking tobacco or marijuana, drinking more than moderately, or obesity—then develop a program to get any and all of these out of your own life. Fourth, seek comradeship in all of this from other members of the family. Make your response to grief a *group* interaction if at all possible and to whatever extent possible. Get professional assistance if needed in these efforts. Most professionals will be elated to hear of such intentions on your part.

You have a right to say: "I thought you were going to talk about *spiritual* health. You have talked about my

physical well-being." You are right! However, I have
simply been specific about spiritual welfare. Paul says that
we are to present our bodies as a sacrifice unto God,
which is our spiritual service. You can do nothing more
spiritual than to maintain your own physical health. Your
body is the temple of the Holy Spirit. You serve God well
if you take care of your body as a means of worshiping
God.

Sudden Death: Suicide

If your loved one's death was a suicide, it is imperative
that you get the full data from the police, who are
routinely called in such cases. Clear up any doubt that it
was indeed a suicide. Lingering doubts about this can
germinate outlandish fantasies as to how the tragedy
actually occurred. Keep in touch with reality, however
harsh it may be. Stay closely in touch with things as they
are. This keeps you in touch with your own healthy self
and enables your prayers to God to be specific, accurate,
and clear.

Furthermore, it is a good thing to have a family
gathering of all who were close to the deceased. Invite
your family physician or a recommended psychiatrist to
confer with you as a group. Ask any questions you feel
like asking. Express in words just how you feel. Another
such gathering could be led by your family pastor. I have
rendered this kind of ministry to families suffering from
the grief over a suicidal death, and I can heartily
encourage this procedure.

You may already be asking: "Is suicide a sin and is it
forgivable?" It is a sin in that the person who does it takes
into his or her own hands prerogatives that belong only to
God. It is forgivable, I believe, because God's love extends
to us in the depths of our despair. Nowhere can I find any

theological basis for describing suicide as an unpardonable sin.

Grief over a suicide is accompanied by more blaming of self and others than is the case with other causes of death. Each person asks: "Am I in some way to blame? What could I have done to prevent this from happening?" Pointing of fingers at other "culprits" is not uncommon after a suicide. The self-reproachings and the accusations get no one anywhere. The basic responsibility belongs to the person who killed himself or herself. I have been impressed upon reading notes left by suicides as to how many of them ask their family members to forgive them. Obviously those who write these notes feel responsible. Whether the deceased asks forgiveness in a suicide or not, no one else can accurately take the blame or blame someone else for it. A wise woman, Virginia Satir, calls this "living in the blame frame." Get out of this frame of mind.

A helpful book has been written with you particularly in mind. John Hewett's *After Suicide* (Westminster Press, 1980) is precisely tailored to give you special guidance. Go to your bookstore and order it, if they do not have it on hand.

Sudden Death: Accidents

If the cause of your loved one's death was an accident, you may be asking: "How could God let a thing like this happen?" This is a natural, abrupt response to God. God hears your question. As a fellow seeker with you, I feel that at the base of this question is an assertion: "God, this is not fair!" No. It is not fair. Yet accidents occur on a "calculated risk" basis. One can accurately say that the automobiles are *the* most hazardous mode of transportation—next to motorcycles, that is. Each time we get in a car, we take a calculated risk much higher than if we ride public transportation. Even airplanes are safer. If we match the risk we take with a prayer for wisdom and defensive driving, then God intervenes through the processes of our own mind. We drive within the speed limit, give the right of way rather than demand it. We refuse to drink alcohol when we are going to drive. We buckle up our seatbelts. We avoid driving in areas with unduly high accident rates. We avoid driving in fog, sleet, snow, and heavy rain. We drive as little at night as we possibly can. We look upon these "driving rituals" as forms of prayer to God for safety in travel. Driving an automobile is a massive responsibility to God and our neighbor. Yet, with the best of devotion, accidents happen. You struggle in your spirit with the unfairness of your loved one's death caused by a reckless or drunken driver, or the sudden loosing of a load of steel pipe on a curve. Such an accident took the life of the daughter of L. D. Johnson, chaplain at Furman University. He has written his own autobiographical story of his grief in his book entitled *The Morning After Death*. He says: "But some accidents just happen. That seems to have been the nature of Carole's accident. It was no less fatal and permanent than if we could have blamed somebody. Could God have prevented it? Yes, since he is God. Why didn't he? I do not know. I live with the mystery. . . . Does God rejoice and weep with us? Yes, I believe he does. . . . Well intentioned platitudes about God knowing best and making no mistakes leave me comfortless, too." He joins a minister of an earlier century, Friedrich Schleiermacher, in praying: "Make even this grievous trial a new blessing for me in my vocation." (L. D. Johnson, *The Morning After Death*, pp. 116-117; Broadman Press, 1978.) I commend this whole book to you.

Sudden Death: Homicide

A pastor was on vacation. He and his wife were called in the middle of the night and told that their oldest son had been murdered. Three men drew a gun on him, forced him into his car. He attempted—apparently—to drive his car to a police station. They shot him in the back and fled. Nothing has been heard now, five years later, as to who committed the murder.

The poignancy of this kind of grief is multiplied many times over in the injustice, hurt, and anger it arouses. The anger of those who grieve spreads from the killers to the seemingly nonchalant law enforcement officers, to the whole world that seems unmoved by their loss.

There is also the temptation to become a detective, to take the law into your own hands. Yet the possibility of meeting your own death as a result of this sleuthing is very high. The persons who did it know who you are, but you don't know who they are. By now they have your name, address, telephone number, and license number. Heroics are tempting, but they can double the grief of the other members of your family and end in your own death.

So—you feel like screaming, not just crying. Find a place and do so! Wise counselors are needed for you and each one of your family. Do not leave the festering pain as is. Go to the counselor of your choice. Yes, you are strong enough to bear it alone. It will take longer. You live in times like those described by Isaiah, who said: "I am a man of unclean lips, and I dwell in the midst of a people of unclean lips." Yet he was more specific than this in speaking of his home country:

> Ah, sinful nation,
>   a people laden with iniquity,
> offspring of evildoers,
>   sons who deal corruptly!

They have forsaken the Lord,
    they have despised the Holy One of Israel,
    they are utterly estranged.

Why will you still be smitten,
    that you continue to rebel?
The whole head is sick,
    and the whole heart faint.
From the sole of the foot even to the head,
    there is no soundness in it,
but bruises and sores
    and bleeding wounds;
they are not pressed out, or bound up,
    or softened with oil.

(Isa. 1:4-6)

The violence that snuffed out your loved one's life is increasingly becoming a way of life for many Americans. The seeds of violence are widespread—poverty, filth, greed, drugs, and murder for hire. The sores of society are great. Possibly out of this suffering of yours can come a sharpened sense of vocation in looking minutely at the self-perpetuation of crime in our penal system—chaos is a better word. The chaplains in prisons could give you useful interpretations of the driving forces that move persons to kill total strangers. Out of the depths of your loss, may some distilled essence of your suffering stay the motives of others to kill someone's son, daughter, father, mother, husband, or wife.

Sudden Infant Death

A certain nurse is a grandmother. She has a daughter whose first child died at birth. She has another daughter whose six-month-old baby was a victim of what is commonly called "crib death," less commonly called "SIDS," or sudden infant death syndrome. Now, three years later, she does not want to talk about this traumatic loss. It is too painful.

The sudden infant death syndrome has existed for many centuries. Its true nature was not recognized until the 1940's. Before this, these deaths of little babies were thought to have been caused by their having been smothered to death in their bedclothes or having been overlaid by the bodies of their parents or siblings sleeping in the same bed. Up until the 1700's, church courts tried the parents for negligence. Later, civil courts did the same. The parents were adjudged to be criminally negligent of their child.

This is not the case today. Modern medicine has a highly developed specialty known as pathology. Pathologists have many duties, one of which is scientifically establishing the cause of death. They have clearly established that smothering is *not* the cause of these sudden infant deaths. They have not yet established what *is* the cause. They have various estimates: an enlarged thymus, an exceptionally small heartbeat, correlations with maternal ages of less than twenty years, a particular type O blood, or viral encephalitis. These are among the variety of possible causes of death found in eleven different studies representing many states in this country, Great Britain, Australia, and New Zealand.

If this mysterious sudden-death syndrome has taken your baby from you, bear in mind that self-blame is natural. You see yourself as a conscientious parent. The whole responsibility of your baby's life was in your hands and it died. Do not let this heavy feeling do away with your good judgment. Hold steady. Ask your physician for the pathology report. You may learn things that will help you assure the health of other children you may have. Without your knowing it, your dead baby may well have been and probably was a high-risk infant from the outset.

I know that this discussion is cold comfort to you, because nothing can bring your baby back to you now. The main thing these facts will do is to strengthen you for the *long run* of your grief. They will dispel some of the mystery and the agony of the unknown. More than that, they will put you in touch with other people. Some of these will be physicians, nurses, and ministers.

You are not alone. Each year an estimated 10,000 healthy, normal babies die suddenly. Sudden infant death centers, such as the one at Minneapolis Children's Health Center, are now in action. A national organization of the bereaved parents has begun. Ask your local department of health if there is one near you. If not, you may contact the national office: National Sudden Infant Death Syndrome Foundation, 310 S. Michigan Avenue, Chicago, Ill.   60604.

4.
No-End Grief

DEATH HAS A FINALITY ALL ITS OWN. JUST AS BIRTH IS A time of beginning afresh for the baby and all those around the newborn, death is an end, a closure. Except in those instances in which a person is assumed to be dead even though the body is never found, death is a clean-cut grief. However, grief is not restricted to death situations, although the patterns of mourning are much the same in any other kind of grief. I have chosen the name "no-end grief" for those griefs which have no predictable time of conclusion. They must be lived with. These kinds of grief can be thought of as the unremitting stress of perpetual sorrow. What prompted the name "no-end grief"? I picked it from a recurring comment of many persons describing their feelings. They would say: "There is just no end to this." Furthermore, I had the question put to me by a neurosurgeon on a panel. He asked: "What kind of grief is it that just keeps going, never lets up, and has to be lived with on a permanent basis?" As he and I struggled for a name, we arrived at "no-end" as the clearest title for this kind of grief.

EXAMPLES OF NO-END GRIEF

Also, a considerable number of other persons presented these repetitive sentences: "Death could not have been this bad." Or, "It would have been easier to bear if she (he) had died." Under these words were a prayer: "How long, O Lord, how long?" Some carefully described examples will clarify what no-end grief is.

Divorce and Children

Grief is by definition a negative experience. Persons going through a divorce rarely use the word "grief" to describe their feelings. Therefore, when I describe divorce as a no-end grief situation, you are likely to feel that I am being negative and unsympathetic toward persons who are divorced. Please! I am not! To the contrary, you probably feel some of the relief that comes to persons who have been through a long, agonizing journey of anticipatory grief described in Chapter 2. What has happened to you is not completely negative. Certainly it is not all positive, either. Grief is one important dimension of divorce. Thinking of it this way may help you to chart the path ahead more surely. Grief over a divorce may be of an anticipatory nature. Or it may have been a sudden, catastrophic experience for you. This does indeed happen. I have seen it often. In either a long-feared divorce or a sudden one, you are facing a no-end grief of a very special kind. The holidays, weddings, funerals, commencements, family dinners, or other special occasions such as the birth date of a grandchild, have a way of "rehearsing" the past events.

Marriages can and do end. There is a finality about a divorce decree. However, if the couple being divorced have children, the divorce can be the beginning of a whole new kind of grief both for the children and for their parents.

Many divorced couples work out creative separate relationships to their children. As many or more do not, and the care and guidance of children continues the struggle. In these instances, grief has no end, it seems.

Marriages are dissolvable in civil courts, but children persist as living epistles of the "one flesh" that once was, at least for that span of ecstasy that brought them into being. As Peter Ustinov said: "Children are the one consistent result of human ecstasy." Therefore, children are particularly vulnerable to our sense, or lack of a sense, of responsibility for following them to their maturity. In a word, grief often goes on and on after a divorce, particularly where there are children. Repetitive incidents occur that re-present the breach of the relationship.

The child, in turn, fantasizes that he or she was, in some unknown way, responsible for the breakup of the marriage. In their childish omnipotence, some children may feel not only responsible for the divorce but also impelled to bring their parents back together again. Yet other children will be relieved that the severe conflict, arguments, and even physical abuse are over.

The parent who spends most of the time with the children bears the brunt of the unending grief. Usually, though not always, it is the mother. Divorce is not only a marital crisis, it is also a financial disaster in many instances. This is particularly true of middle- and upper-class families. The family may be also bereaved of their former security. They suffer from having to pull up their roots and move. They grieve over their separation from friends and schoolmates as well. Both the man and the woman in a divorce are thrust back into the single state again. In a couple-oriented church and social life, they are inadvertently, at times, and intentionally, at other times, left out of social gatherings.

The major hazard in a postdivorce grief experience is undue haste to repair the damage. The initial shock, numbing, and disbelief that the break has happened often do not have time to wear off before one or the other partner (or both) hastens into another marriage. In one's fantasy about restoring a happy marriage, one may choose a mate to "replace" the previous partner rather than take the time both to grieve adequately and to come to know a new partner as a person in her or his own right.

In the face of this subtle kind of peril, let me urge you, if these comments strike a familiar chord with you, to stand fast for a while. Push ahead with the same routines in your church to which you have been accustomed. Hold steady to your course. If the church has a reasonably large membership, you will soon meet others in your same situation. One woman teamed up with a woman lawyer to provide a financial planning ministry for recently divorced women. Another has been a moving spirit in the organization of a Sunday school class for "formerly marrieds." The wisdom of Proverbs is the way to manage this kind of unshared grief:

> Let your eyes look directly forward,
>   and your gaze be straight before you.
> Take heed to the path of your feet,
>   then all your ways will be sure.
> Do not swerve to the right or to the left;
>   turn your foot away from evil.
>   (Prov. 4:25-27)

In brief, maintain your own integrity. Be engrossed in a keen sense of vocation about your work, your parenthood, and your participation in a fellowship of believers. Hold steady to your course. You will find many other perpetually sorrowing persons to whom you will be a comfort.

Physical Handicaps

In many accidents the victims are not killed. Instead, they are handicapped for the rest of their lives. Their possibilities of living a normal life-span are high, given the right kind of rehabilitation and family support. Therefore, instead of a sudden-death grief syndrome, a no-end grief situation comes into being.

From my clinical involvement within a large university medical center I have met several families undergoing such stress. Their experience at one point or another may coincide with yours.

Automobile accidents are probably the most common source of these injuries. A twenty-year-old man, on his way home from a party with a group of friends in his car, was struck head on by a pickup truck. All of his passengers were uninjured except for minor cuts and bruises. However, his spine was damaged and the spinal cord irreversibly injured, leaving him paralyzed from the rib cage down. His father, who refuses to accept what has happened, insists that his son will once again walk.

Motorcycle accidents are a common source of multiple and irreversible damage to the central nervous system, often because of brain injuries.

Sports accidents in football, skiing, etc., create no-end grief situations in too many cases. A seventeen-year-old boy was playing football and enjoying life to the fullest. In one play in which he was tackled, he fell on his head and snapped his spinal cord at the base of his neck. He will always be paralyzed from his neck down. His parents' whole lives, as well as his, must be reorganized around this handicap. It is a no-end loss.

Stroke patients, usually but not always in their later maturity, lose capabilities such as sight, hearing, walking, and talking. Memory may be grossly impaired. A man fifty-five years old now sits in one place in his house until his wife, who is on 24-hour nursing duty for him, moves him to another. He has one sentence of communicable conversation: "I sit here all day and think about how things used to be and never will be again."

The grief over the lost function is perpetual. Granted that memory remains intact, the treasured memory of events *before* the loss can continue to enrich your life. Get to the point that you can muster the courage to take advantage of the memory treasure. For example, a blind person can remember what colors are. The wonderful world of color from memory can be accompanied by feeling—by touching objects.

Furthermore, you will notice "compensation." Ralph Waldo Emerson wrote an essay entitled simply "Compensation." Alfred Adler described this phenomenon, noting that when one eye was lost, the other eye "made up for" its lost function. If persons lose their eyesight, the senses of smell, touch, and hearing tend to become more acutely active. One way of offsetting the sense of helplessness in persons affected by an accident or a stroke, and in yourself if you are their loved one, is to push this compensatory power to the outer limits. Seek the spiritual discipline to develop the significant, useful, *surviving* gifts of the handicapped instead of wallowing in immobilizing grief over what is lost.

Speaking of "helplessness," the great temptation of the physically handicapped is simply to give up, give in, and allow the real assets and skills they have left to go undeveloped. These atrophy or "waste away" from disuse. The staff of a modern rehabilitation center for the physically handicapped is unrelenting in its instruction, demand, and support toward a patient's becoming as independent as possible.

The temptation of family and friends is to help the person more than is needed. What discipline it takes for a father or mother to *let* their handicapped daughter operate her own wheelchair rather than push it *for* her! You must remember that mother and father knew her as an infant! They tend to regress *with* her and want to baby her. The toilsome disciplines of no-end grief have outstanding rewards for them, however, when they see her once again going from place to place alone without help.

I hope I have introduced a creative response to the no-end grief of seeing your family member permanently handicapped. Jan Cox-Gedmak, a very sensitive and caring chaplain at the Institute of Physical Medicine and Rehabilitation in Louisville, Kentucky, has written a vivid documentary about the inner world of physically handicapped persons and their families entitled *Coping with Physical Disability* (Westminster Press, 1980). You will find this one of the most useful and inexpensive guides available, as well as accurately empathic and genuinely helpful to you on the journey ahead.

In one sense, the physically handicapped person has the same problem as those who have full use of their bodies: accepting limitations. None of us is expert at knowing our limits, working within them, and pushing the limits back just a bit for freedom's sake. The physically handicapped person has had this problem raised to the nth degree and is always aware of it. We rarely are.

Furthermore, the longer all of us live, the more handicaps we develop. Hearing, seeing, moving, walking, eating, and sleeping are abilities we assume remain forever young. Not so. We gradually lose many functions, many of them through disuse. We do not die all at once, but piece by piece. This we share with the physically handicapped. They are ourselves "writ large."

Yet we share a common faith, also, that the indwelling power of the Holy Spirit gives us courage and vitalizes the totality of our being to rise above its incompleteness when we are *wholeheartedly* dedicated to a calling from God. The complex factors of severe limitation and wholehearted commitment are held in balance by the indwelling Spirit of God. Handicap and limitation are embraced by grace. Yet that same grace summons us to comfort others as we have been comforted by God.

Birth Defects and/or Mental Retardation

Every Wednesday I spend a good part of the day working within a staff of eight different specialties in the Child Evaluation Center of the Department of Pediatrics of our School of Medicine. We carefully assess the complex data found in extensive examination, care, and observation of *one* child who is suffering from a hereditary, congenital, or birth-injury defect. Or the child may be mentally retarded and yet physically fit. We get to know the parents. They yearn to be able now to *make* their child achieve more than is possible. They are tempted to overprotect the child, and often feel responsible for their child's deficiency. An overwhelming sense of grief and mourning comes to them when they finally can accept that their child will always be limited. A wide range of medical procedures, therapies (such as speech and language therapies), school programs for special education, and both governmental and church institutions are available to stretch the limits of the child to the farthest reach. The task of our staff is to bolster the parents' morale, provide a clear diagnosis, and put the parents in touch with the treatment and educational resources nearest to them.

Yet these parents and siblings are faced with the disciplines of a no-end grief. Many of these children live a normal life-span, i.e., they will probably outlive their parents. At each juncture of the family cycle from birth to old age the well-being of this one child must be reassessed. Some people handle this grief with an integrity and character that comes only through patience and endurance. Others are overwhelmed by the experience. As in the other kinds of no-end grief situations, they endure heavy struggles of the soul.

Major Struggles of the Soul in No-End Grief

Something about the human spirit prompts us in any adversity or ecstasy of life to ask: "How long?" If no end is in sight or promised, we tend to make an end of our own. This is a creative tendency; yet it can run amok, go out of field, or, as we say in our daily speech, "jump the track." Then ensue major struggles of the soul in no-end grief. Some of the struggles I have been a part of in fellowship with people I have known are described below.

The Struggle Not to Abandon the Loved One

One great temptation of the individual members of a family, especially where there is a grossly malformed child or a severe handicap from an accident, is simply to abandon the person. One member of a family may "stand hitched" in pulling the load of caring for another semi-helpless family member. Other members will "ditch" their responsibility altogether. They go about their own concerns *as if* nothing had happened. Occasionally, the whole family does this. They may

commit the person to an institution such as a mental
retardation facility, a rehabilitation center, a nursing
home, or even a state hospital and not visit, help pay
expenses, or anything else. Thus these agencies of the
community become "warehouses" for the unwanted. It is
easy to condemn harshly people who abandon handicapped persons. But it takes more wisdom to enter into
the struggle they face. Their energies and resources
become exhausted. Their coping measures fail. Their
alarm remains uninterrupted. Their judgment becomes
impaired. Their actions are the counsels of their
desperation. The whole family as a working system
grinds to a halt. Consequently, not just the handicapped
person needs support, affection, and relief from despair.
The whole family does.

If you and your family are caught up in this kind of
desperation, you can do something to meet *all* your needs
and not just those of one member. The Family Service
organization is a national program of family care. It has
centers in cities of moderate size all over the United
States. These centers are locally supported by United
Fund, United Way, or Community Chest funds. In my
city, the Family Service agency is listed under the name
"Family and Children's Agency" in the telephone book.
Ask for help in working out a plan that takes into
consideration the needs of the handicapped member,
and those of all the rest of you as well. Some more even
distribution of responsibility is an absolute necessity.
Then, the family therapists on their staff can use their
specialized skills to develop a just, merciful, and loving
pattern of action.

If, indeed, you cannot find a Family Service agency,
you may well call the nearest medical center and ask for
one of the following persons: the chaplain, or the head of
the department of family practice, or the head of the

department of psychiatry. Present your situation and ask for directions as to where or how you can get family therapy in this crisis.

You will be concerned about financing such an effort. The people I have suggested usually work on a "sliding scale," adjusting their fees in terms of your income, the number in your family, and your eligibility for insurance coverage. Do not let financial insecurity keep you from making these plans. Many times you have not because you ask not. Asking is free, in this instance.

My prayer is that as you struggle to distribute your load of responsibility, you will find in your own community able servants of the common good to share your burden with you. You need not bear it alone. You need not have the memory that you abandoned a handicapped loved one. The way is *through* the trouble, not *out* of it. Be of good courage!

The Struggle with Rage

The injustice of your situation, the frustration of your best efforts and hopes for your loved one, and the hurt that has to be endured all add up to rage. A nameless, speechless, unreasoning demon grips you. You fear losing control of this rage.

In a moment of sheer fatigue the loved one who is handicapped does a trivial but thoughtless thing like spilling a cup of soup on you. You "fly off the handle" and strike out in anger. The horrible thought crosses your mind: "Why don't you die? I could kill you!" Then you are deluged with despair, self-recrimination, and feelings of worthlessness. One mother of a severely retarded child said: "I suddenly felt the urge to kill him. I threw him across the room. Thank God he was not really hurt. But I went to confession as soon as I could and sought forgiveness for my thoughts. I asked God to give me strength, now that I know this temptation, never to give in to it again. My priest was kind and understanding. He assured me of God's forgiveness and God's presence with me."

May you find that kind of understanding in your struggle with rage as you offer it up to God.

The Struggle with Despair

Some people take all their rage out on themselves, not on others. You may be the kind of person that falls into self-condemnation. Not only do you have the care of your loved ones; you also struggle with your own mood of despair. You find yourself getting little sleep, even when you have plenty of opportunity for it. Instead, you sleep lightly, awaken easily, turn and toss, and sleep will not return. Finally, after two or three hours of this, you doze off into a dazed kind of sleep. The time comes to get up. You face another day that looks harsh, bleak, and uninviting.

Furthermore, you have lost much of your appetite for food, for intimate sexual union with your partner, and for all pleasurable events. In addition to this, you feel tired. You drag yourself from one duty to another.

Worst of all, you may be tired of living and see your own death as the only honorable way to terminate the no-end anguish you feel.

If these signs of despair are yours, even two or three of them, you should do one thing immediately. Call your physician, make an appointment, take this book with you, and confess that you are depressed and need help. Your physician can treat your sleep disorder, your mood disorder, and your appetite disorder.

Then, I suggest that you seek out your pastor, or a

pastor whom a friend can commend to you. Ask for spiritual guidance in rebuilding your inner resources of the spirit. Raise any questions you have about God's providence in your own and your loved one's life. Ask to be introduced to other people in the congregation. You and they can "bear one another's burdens, and so fulfil the law of Christ" (Gal. 6:2). Band together in a regular fellowship of prayer, searching for ways to solve practical problems in caring for your loved one. Another national organization of groups like this is The Compassionate Friends. Search your area and see if there is such a group near you. If not, write to the following address for information as to how to get one started: The Compassionate Friends, National Headquarters, P.O. Box 1347, Oak Brook, Ill.   60521.

Once you have begun to *do* the things I have suggested, your feelings of helplessness and isolation will begin to subside. Your despair will tend to loosen its grip. Life will have shafts of light to contrast with the gloom. You have not brought your handicapped loved one's handicap to an end, but you have brought your own despair to an end. By the grace of God, you can exchange your mourning for the oil of gladness, your weary spirit for a garment of praise. (See Isa. 61:1-3.)

The Struggle of Marital Distancing

If you are married and the handicapped person is your child, you may notice that you and your spouse *grieve differently* as you cope with no-end grief. For example, a husband may lose himself in a great deal of work. He may be speechless and seemingly angry inside. He may avoid leaning on *any*one, which includes his wife. The wife, to the contrary, may focus quite completely on around-the-clock nursing attention to the impaired child. She may be quite verbal in expressing her feelings. She may readily reach out to friends and depend upon her pastor or physician. The husband may want none of this, although he may be unconcerned about the time his wife spends talking with others.

These two different ways of grieving soon create much spiritual distance between the husband and wife. I call this "marital distancing," one of the major hazards of the interminable grief and stress related to caring for the injured, the impaired, the handicapped child.

One of the first things you can do about this marital distancing is to recognize and affirm that you are each reacting *differently* to the same great pain you both feel. You each have your own particular grief. Ask whether you can give each other the *right* to be different. If so, each can start "taking lessons" from the other in the particular strengths that the other's own particular way of grief can offer. For example, the mother tends to become *too* absorbed in the child to the neglect of everything else. She *needs* to attend to *some* of "everything else." The father tends to become absorbed in "everything else" and to leave the care of the handicapped person to his wife. He needs to take his turn. Learning how to see to it that the car is serviced and repaired is a skill needed by a mother. Learning how to handle a urethral catheter is a skill needed by a father. Much of the marital distancing arises out of getting stuck with a fixed and biased stereotype of what men are "supposed to do" and what women are "supposed to do." Break out of these stereotypes and trade skills!

Another antidote for marital distancing is to interrupt the stress of caring for the impaired loved one. The no-end grief may be "for the duration," as was said while World War II was going on. However, the stress of the day-to-day care of the loved one *can* be interrupted. A time of rest and recreation—"R and R," as it was called during the Vietnam War—can be planned. Even if it is for only 72 hours, the restoration of your husband-wife relationship is a prime necessity. You *need* each other. Such an interruption gives you tender, private access to each other. You will discover, also, that the impaired family member needs a change also, some privacy, and a respite from both parents.

If one or the other marital partner *is* the impaired one, another kind of marital distancing takes place. Jan Cox-Gedmark's book, *Coping with Physical Disability,* explores thoroughly the forces at work in each of your minds to wedge you apart in the struggle of your souls in this no-end grief. Previous marital rifts may reoccur and widen. Added to this are feelings of guilt and worthlessness. The impaired spouse may assume that the mate has a *right* to walk out. He or she may even prod, aggravate, and urge the spouse to do so. On the other hand, the spouse who is unimpaired physically may not be able to take it any longer, after the passage of much time. The spouse may develop a double life—one that faithfully cares for the handicapped spouse; another in which work, or a clandestine love affair, nourishes personal needs that require care as well.

Whatever shape the marital distancing takes, outside, independent ventilation of your feelings to a counselor, chaplain, pastor, physician, social worker, or psychologist provides both of you with a transfusion of personal strength enabling you both to look at your darkest feelings and to develop a balanced perspective. The most critical distancing can be anticipated and prevented by carefully developing additional sources of wisdom and good judgment.

The Struggle Against Bitterness

Some people respond to perpetual sorrow by being embittered. Perpetual sorrow is certainly not the *only* provocation of bitterness. Nevertheless it deserves attention here.

The struggle against bitterness itself is a battle that is perpetual and never finally won. I can identify with you if this struggle of the soul is yours. The impact of the Vietnam War on our country, our schools, and my family was a long patriotic exercise in futility and cynicism. We are grateful to God every day to know that our elder son went through nearly two years of combat with the Naval Inshore Assault Group and suffered no permanent damage to his body and no impairment of his psychological functioning. However, he *missed* many valuable opportunities and privileges in that long span of time. These opportunities and privileges are the birthright of every young person. This is a bitter pill for me as a father to swallow.

Yet he was extremely fortunate as contrasted with young men in their early thirties whom we see in our psychiatric clinics. As one recently said: "I learned a remarkable skill in the Marines that has *no* marketable value in the civilian job sector: being a sniper with a high-powered rifle with a telescopic sighting device." The severe burden of bitterness of this large segment of our population—Vietnam combat veterans—is a world of pain only now being faced and dealt with by the homes and institutions of our land.

The no-end grief that these veterans and their families experience is saturated with bitterness. As another veteran said to me: "We are the lost generation." Twenty-five hundred of them are literally lost. They or their dead bodies still remain in Southeast Asia. Neither their government nor their families know *whether* they are dead or alive. The endless sorrow of these men's families is poignant testimony to my conviction that their particular grief is unique to them. They bear this open-ended grief alone with little or no spiritual support from either the government or the church. The crowd has really thinned out for them. Bitterness is their portion.

Divorced persons are a much larger group of bereaved persons with a uniquely perpetual grief. The struggle against bitterness among divorced persons takes many forms, both obvious and subtle.

Divorce not only severs the marriage bond; it also devastates the economy of the family. Among the very wealthy this may or may not be so. Among the affluent lower upper class, the middle class, and even skilled labor groups, the financial problems of divorce are almost catastrophic. Therefore, a man or a woman accustomed to the benefits of a comfortable income may be forced to live on the outer fringes of poverty.

A man, for example, who turns over to his divorced wife and their children the house he and his wife have worked years to pay for and lives in a small apartment with little or no equipment may feel bitter through and through. A woman who was accustomed to working prior to the divorce discovers how little her salary is when matched alone against the pile of bills that keep coming. She may formerly have worked by choice but now works out of sheer necessity. Worse than this is the predicament of the woman who has spent most of her adult years as a housewife and mother but now has to enter a male-biased job market with no specific skills. Her pain and loss may all too easily ferment into the vinegar of bitterness.

On another count, marital partners who divorce often have the fantasy that they each can readily find another

partner with whom they can be blissfully happy. Yet after
the divorce they may discover that a married extramarital
partner who seemed ready to take the same step chooses
not to divorce the present husband or wife. Or they may
discover the scarcity of eligible mates. Those that are
available, scarce as their number may be, often are not
highly suitable people for a variety of reasons. When one
divorced spouse does not readily find a new mate, but the
other quickly remarries, then the unfairness of one's
plight quickly turns the spirit sour. Loneliness aggravates
the bitterness all the more.

Bitterness too often leads to a set of plans to "get even,"
to retaliate. A pattern of willful behavior comes into
being. For example, if there are children in the divorced
family, punishing "strike backs" may come when things
are done to prevent the divorced spouse from seeing,
visiting, or talking by telephone with his or her children.
When a visitation schedule is set, delaying procedures
passively obstruct the happiness of those occasions.
Consciously spiteful and revengeful things are done to
harass the divorced spouse. The tragedy falls most
heavily on the children. They become pawns in the chess
game of revenge.

The critical spiritual problem in the struggle against
bitterness is this: You are being tempted to place a severe
experience such as the Vietnam War, a tragic divorce, or
the murder of one of your loved ones *at the center* of your
whole life. This is idolatry. Only God can safely, wisely,
and lovingly be at the center of our lives. Anyone or
anything which is less than God and which is placed at the
center—whether for reasons of love or hate—begins to
exercise demonic, possessive power over us. We are
consumed by that idol. Our spiritual discipline—both
yours and mine—is to cast down every high thing that
exalts itself against our primary relation to God, the

supreme devotion of our lives. This temptation is not obvious. It is subtle, and thus all the more difficult to name and to conquer.

But *you* will be different. You will face it for what it is. By God's grace you are going to recover from the bitterness of your no-end grief.

5.

Near-Miss Grief

MIRACLES OCCUR OFTEN WHEN YOU WORK WITH BEREAVED PEOPLE. The apostle Paul and Luke the beloved physician who accompanied him were in a boat close inshore off the island of Crete. A northeaster struck the sea. They were so violently storm-tossed that they began to throw cargo overboard. Luke tells us:

> And when neither sun nor stars appeared for many a day, and no small tempest lay on us, all hope of our being saved was at last abandoned. (Acts 27:20)

Paul assured them that they would *not* lose their lives, even though they would endure shipwreck. Not a hair of their heads would perish, he said. They ate bread and gave thanks. The ship was wrecked, but all escaped safely to land. The whole story in Acts 27 tells of a gripping encounter with almost certain death, from which they were delivered. Modern examples of such deliverance from death may help in characterizing your particular grief.

You ask this question: "How best can we describe that kind of grief in which a person was as good as dead, but by some means is delivered from such a fate? For all practical purposes, he or she will now live out a normal life expectancy." As I have thought of instances in which this has actually happened, several phrases came to mind: "close shave," "narrow escape," "hair's breadth," "miraculous deliverance," "spontaneous recovery." As time went on, I continued to tug at the idea. I associated it with military combat. The terms "direct hit" and "near miss" took root in my thinking. I settled upon "near-miss grief" as a name. I have had close friends, as well as our own son, describe how they narrowly escaped from a "near-miss" explosion in combat. Then I have repeatedly seen individuals and families mysteriously delivered from destruction. The grief they experience is unique, a qualitatively different kind of grief.

Examples of Near-Miss Grief

Your particular grief may be of this kind. Other kinds of grief I have described may, for that reason, not fit your situation. The following detailed discussion may touch you where you are. What are some of the events that flow together to cause near-miss grief?

A Wrong Diagnosis of a Fatal Disease

The possibility of cancer weighs upon you repeatedly as you read your newspaper and listen to television and radio. This and that kind of food, drug, or contaminant of the air, earth, or water is pronounced "carcinogenic," i.e., a possible cause of cancer. Then one day you are admitted to a hospital. After elaborate tests, you are told that you have cancer. Then days, weeks, months later, you are told that this was a wrong diagnosis. Some malfunction of diagnostic equipment or some technical mistake was made. Or, sometime after that diagnosis, a more accurate and useful kind of equipment is used that yields better results in diagnosis. Or a real human error was made, such as confusing *your* test results with those of someone else, which gave another's diagnosis to you and yours to someone else. These fluke misadventures are rare, but they do happen. Such a thing happened to me because of a foul-up by a highly competent (and greatly embarrassed) medical staff. I have also seen it happen with psychiatric patients who were wrongly diagnosed. Dramatic discoveries in diagnostic procedures are making it possible to improve drastically on the precision of diagnosis and treatment of mental patients. Still, mistakes do occur.

The crucial question you should ask youself if you or your loved one has received a "doomsday" diagnosis is: "*When* was the last diagnosis?" If it was over a year ago, you deserve a new look at your situation.

If you do discover that you have been wrongly diagnosed, you then have a tremendous readjustment to make. You now have years of life expectancy rather than the expectation of death in the near future. Illness has its social and spiritual side effects. Not all of them are bad. Being the center of attention, being the controlling force in your family, being free of some of the demands of life, are things all too easy to find acceptable. When they settle into habits, they are equally difficult to give up. Giving them up is a test of character. Under God's inspiration you will, I pray, rise to the test and have done with what really are no longer useful but have become harmful ways of living. You want and need to be a fully functioning adult.

Right Diagnosis/New Cure

Physicians do not speak of "terminal" illness; they speak of "incurable" disorders. Leukemia, for example, has been an incurable disorder for a long time. More recently therapies have been discovered whereby some kinds of leukemia, previously incurable, are now curable.

A physician who specializes in leukemia in children and youth, Donald Kmetz, M.D., recently told me of eleven families who were advised that a child of theirs with leukemia would live only a short time. During the process of these children's illness, methods of curing them have been discovered, tested, and proved. Now, he says, the families of these children, as well as the children themselves, are having to "reprogram" their whole lives around the assumption that this child will live out a normal life expectancy. Imagine the sense of deliverance, the feeling of a close encounter with a tragic death, the feeling of having barely escaped, the sense of a "near miss." Can the family ever get over treating the child preferentially? When the son or daughter is sixteen or twenty and ready to leave the home, will the parents still clutch onto their child for fear something dreadful will happen? In short, how can they ever shift back to a normal handling of this child's needs? Working through this test of character is made stickier and more difficult by a "sweet, sweet sentimentality." Stooping to sentimentality and wallowing in nostalgia is easy. Celebrating, debriefing, giving thanks to God in the face of such a discovery takes months of hard personal discipline. The years ahead, however, require having done with this event and "getting on with life" in the present and the future. The main gift is the savoring of each day for its own sake and thanking God that all things have been made anew.

Correct Diagnosis/Wrong Reaction

Occasionally a person will come down with a chronic disease that is uncomfortable. Its treatments are simple, but must become a part of the person's way of life from now on. If these treatments are followed religiously, the person can live a reasonably normal life. Some examples of this are diabetes, epilepsy, hemochromatosis (too much iron in the blood).

The fate of having a chronic disorder may throw the patient into the kind of depression that prompts a person to predict his or her own immediate death. One's lifework grinds to a halt; relationships to the marital partner become strained and break; and one falls back on one's family of origin, i.e., parents and siblings. Such a patient is out of touch with reality, but is not definably mentally ill. Yet he or she has the whole family in an uproar periodically. These crises boil down to a question of who is going to finance a purely inactive and immobilized way of life. Pushed to extremes, the critical issues are: Is this person willing to work? and Where and with whom shall the patient live?

The trauma of discovering the chronic disease started a pattern of helplessness that the patient does not rally to break. You may have had this kind of grief happen to you. At first you thought you would die; then you learned that instead you would be subjected to the disciplines of medication, regular medical testing, and treatment. You cannot accept this persistent demand for personal discipline. Its rituals serve only to remind you of your loss of perfect health. The "near miss" of death left you chronically impaired. You cannot convey your loss of energy, the confusion of your life purpose, and the meaning of life itself. Once you thought you would soon die; now you must keep on living. For what? Your dreams of what you might have been or what you expect immediately to happen keep you from taking the first simple steps toward personal independence, responsible work, and small achievements faithfully completed.

Your major problem is that of accepting as your own the boredom, the fatigue, and the occasional pointlessness of many of the jobs within your reach. You are not an exception to these banes of human existence. Everybody started somewhere and stayed with a job until able to move to something better. Do not let the discovery of this limiting disorder be the center of your existence. In short, do not worship your disorder! God only is adequate for your worship! Though your deliverance from the power of your disorder was partial, nevertheless God has put the means in your hands to push it out of the center of your life.

Near-Miss Accidents

Newscasts tell us of a fatal fire in New York State in which many people were killed. Earlier a hotel in Las Vegas burned; nearly a hundred persons were killed and many more injured. One man who was in *both* fires escaped each of them unharmed! To say that he leads a "charmed life" would be a superstitious way to explain this. I wonder what *his* explanation would be. How did he react to this double deliverance?

The jarring realization of how fragile life is, how we live in risk at all times, comes to us when we read stories like this. If you have gone through such a nightmare and come out alive and whole, you are saying: "I came through it, but I'll never be the same again." You won't, either. Some people change by rededicating their lives to the service and worship of God. They feel that God's providence requires that they live the liberated life. Even this, though, can make the memory of the terror central in your life. You relive again and again each minute detail of the event. Doing so hinders your putting the experience in the past. Like a creeping kudzu vine, this memory covers your whole life function. You get stuck in that moment in time. Now your prayer is for deliverance from the *memory* of the accident. Such a need is especially apparent if this kind of preoccupation plagues you to the point of interfering permanently with your work, your family relationships, and your friendships with people you value outside your family. If this persists three to six months after the accident, then you will do well to consult with your pastor, your physician, or someone else whom you would appoint as your counselor.

Combat/Concentration Camp Trauma

Conditions of war present some of the heaviest stress known to humankind. Combat veterans are often the epitome of near-miss grief. If you are such a veteran, you may well have memories of narrow escapes in which you survived but your comrades in battle were killed or severely wounded. Remember that the term "near miss" comes from military combat. The whole metaphor fits your particular grief better than that of many other people.

You have deep feelings that breed loneliness for you. Not many of the civilians you know have *anything* in their range of experience that ties in with what you went through. You may think that discussing your grief with them—regardless of how much they love you—is futile. They have nothing with which to compare your grief. The end result is that you just don't pour out your grief to anyone. It stays pent up within you. You don't wear the combat experience as a chance to tell old war stories at every turn of the way. You grieve in silence, not only at repeated tragedies you went through, and comrades you saw killed, but also at the way your own life was impeded, rerouted, and reshaped by all that precious time in a war.

As you read this, you may not be the combat veteran himself. You are his relative. He has a whole inner world about which you can only guess. You have asked specific questions in the past and gotten a brief, unrevealing answer. Yet you wonder if this person whom you love is aware of your heartfelt need to share his grief. Maybe if the two of you read this section of this book together it would strike a spark of understanding that will ignite conversation between you.

You as a relative of a combat veteran may have experienced with him a unique kind of near-miss grief. He was held a prisoner of war for many months, even years. You may have given him up for dead. Then he was released and returned home. The unspeakable no-end grief is now reshaped into a near-miss kind of grief. You and he are aware that many others are probably still sweating out the endless grief that their loved one is still absent—whether dead or alive they know not. Why has reunion come for you and not them?

The taking of hostages seems to be increasingly a factor in the troubled times in which we live. A whole nation may be caught up in what seems to be a grief with no discernible end. This grief controls and biases many other hurting concerns of the American people. The plight of the nation is mild in contrast with the feelings of the hostages and their families. When several hostages are released before others, how do they cope with the fact that they are free and their colleagues are still being held? In their deliverance, how do they rebuild their lives after this traumatic disruption of their lives?

The conditions of life that hostages suffer are a poignant blend of first a no-end grief and then a near-miss grief. The thought that death itself might be easier to bear than this interminable suspended animation may occur often to both the hostages and their families. This thought is the negative, harsh side of what on its positive and loving side is a prayer: "How long, O Lord, how long?" The consolation of God, it seems, is in his revelation of the just and loving end to this grief.

Yet the very act of deliverance itself relieves stress dramatically. How to get on with life without letting this "near miss" of destruction dominate their remaining years is the problem of hostages everywhere upon being released.

COMMON THEMES OF NEAR-MISS GRIEF

Time would fail us to enumerate all the occasions of near-miss grief. However, some common themes appear in each particular instance. Persons so affected suffer *in isolation* more than is true of most grief situations. The immediate occasion of deliverance may give rise to a short-lived celebration on the part of the larger community. There is no funeral in near-miss grief. The thinning of the crowd is abrupt and final. You are left with the nightmarish memories that plague your days and saturate your dreams at night. You become isolated in this grief very quickly. Therefore, it is imperative that, just as quickly as possible, you pick out a friend as confidant or a professional counselor with whom you can converse about the fallout of memories and feelings that continues without inter-ruption. I hope you can call upon a trusted and beloved pastor. For example, a tornado struck the immediate community where I live. Our home was not in the path of it; only nearby. The homes of hundreds were destroyed. The pastor of a church in the devastated area conducted a continuous "debriefing group" for the next eighteen months. Persons who had continuing

buildups of feeling about the tragedy were encouraged
to be a part of this group. I think that some kind of
continuing care at the individual, family, and group
levels should be provided for survivors of other such
tragedies. Though these people are alive, their lives are
drastically altered. The people of God have a responsibility in providing spiritual meaning to people amid
catastrophe. You can catalyze such a group. Discuss it
with your pastor, who may know others like you who
can form a fellowship of suffering and hope.

An Acute Sense of Being Delivered

The Lord delivers us from destruction. God lifts us
from the pit. The Lord reaches down into our "land of
bondage" and delivers us from bondage. God gives us a
new kind of freedom. In both the Old Testament (see
Deut. 5:12-15) and the New Testament (Gal. 4:21 to
5:1), deliverance from bondage is, beyond God's acts of
creation, a primary gift of Providence.

However, people today are generally not schooled in
a larger and deeper knowledge of the Old and New
Testaments. Hence, when a near-miss grief comes upon
them, they do not readily associate their own plight with
that of the Hebrew people. In any case, you can find the
fellowship of the heroes of faith briefly described in
such a passage as Heb. 11:29-40.

If you are one who struggles to see some rhyme and
reason, some pattern of interpretation larger and better
than your bitterness at the tragedy that befell you, then
you will find company with the people of the Old and
New Testaments. To them their deliverance was an
unmistakable sign of God's favor and providence. Take
the painful memories of your tragedy and expose them
to the books of Deuteronomy, Galatians, and Hebrews.

Read each book rapidly, as you would read a newspaper. Get an overview of their messages of deliverance. Then go back and underline specific verses that speak to your condition. Your deliverance from destruction need no longer lack a clear meaning under God.

A Vague Sense of Shame

Your deliverance from destruction may cause you to think of other people near you in the tragedy who did *not* make it. They were killed. You mourn their death. Yet you are alive and well and have the rest of your life on your hands. Why you and not them? Whatever feelings of worthlessness you have within you come to the fore and fill you with a vague sense of shame. You may have bargained with God while the tragic events were happening. Now you are immobilized by a sense of depression. You wonder what you can say or how you can *undo* the damage you and the families of the dead comrades have suffered.

A Fresh Sense of Calling and Vocation

You need not be overwhelmed by the sense of shame I have just mentioned. The need to undo the tragedy has in it the germinating seeds of a fresh sense of calling and vocation. Fyodor Dostoevsky, the Russian novelist, was a prisoner of the Czar in his day. He was condemned to death by the firing squad. He had no way out of the death sentence. He was led out to be shot. Just as he was to be killed—the soldiers had their guns loaded, shouldered, and cocked to fire—the emperor issued a reprieve. Dostoevsky, commenting later in his novel *The Idiot,* wrote: "What an eternity! What if I did not die. All eternity would be mine. Oh, then I would change every minute into a century; I would not lose a single one; I would keep track of all my instincts, and would not spend any of them lightly."

A contemporary example of such a discovery of a new purpose in life is Jeremiah Denton, a Vietnam veteran who spent years in a North Vietnamese prison camp before being released. He has returned to America, run for the United States Senate, and been elected. You and I can draw inspiration from watching his career in the next several years.

You yourself have, in the brutal tragedy from which you have been delivered, the raw materials of a whole new reason to live. You can now write a whole new chapter in the book of your life. I pray that you may soon find specific shape for your feeling of destiny. Then you can say with Joseph in Egypt, to all who would have worked your destruction from which you have been delivered:

> As for you, you meant evil against me; but God meant it for good, to bring it about that many people should be kept alive, as they are today. So do not fear; I will provide for you and your little ones. (Gen. 50:20-21)

The Temptation to Bitterness

In the throes of your grief work, your major test of character will be the temptation to fall back into bitterness that such a fate turned out to be yours. Consumed as you are with the unfairness of it all, the fact that you are alive and reasonably well is cold comfort. You rehearse the event and imagine what might have been had it not happened. The whole memory becomes the center of an embittered self. The great conviction I suggest to you is that you owe yourself something better than this. You can have faith that God is larger and more loving than to make this event the controlling power in life. Centering your life on the tragedy turns the powers of your life over to the past and its "curse character." May you resist this with a whole heart and draw the line immediately in reasserting your basic freedom under God.

6.
Grieving But Staying Well

YOU HAVE LOST A TREASURED PERSON IN YOUR LIFE. YOU MUST TAKE all needed wise measures not to let this loss cause you to lose your health. Your grief *can* itself become an illness. That is a hazard. You can avoid it. You can stay well. The tests of character by grief are unrelenting. Not all people find it in themselves to withstand the toll of grief on their health and well-being. There are those for whom grief becomes something contrary to the intention of God and the way God has created us. Instead of being a process that has its work and is done, grief becomes a way of life. In these instances, it interferes with their work, their love life, and their friendships with others. Even their relationship to God is hindered and distorted. With the help of good counsel and by the power of God in your life, you can stay well.

GRIEF AND ITS NORMAL PROCESS

Grief is a normal depression. It is healthy when one moves through a definite pattern of behaviors and states of consciousness. In Chapter 2, I described some of these behaviors (or rituals) and states of consciousness. In the succeeding chapters I described special kinds of grief situations. Generally speaking, you move through the following mental and emotional states in a time frame that varies from three or four months to two or three years:

Stage One: Shock. The impact of the initial news of the loss leaves you in shock. For a more detailed description of shock, refer to the discussion in Chapter 3.

Stage Two: Numbness. In a dazed condition, you attend only to the practical necessities of the funeral, meeting those who would console you and interacting with relatives, especially those who have not been seen recently.

Stage Three: The Struggle Between Fantasy and Reality. It takes time to associate things, people, events, and the delicate routines of life with the harsh reality of your loss. Great areas of your less conscious thinking continue to respond *as if* your loved one were still alive. During sleep you may dream that he or she is alive. Often the dream awakens you. Then you know it is not so.

Stage Four: Acceptance of Reality. This shows itself in exhaustion, tears of helplessness, and a normal time of depression. Pouring out your grief to a friend, an intimate relative, your pastor, your physician, and in your prayers is a great necessity. Let yourself go in such a time as this.

Stage Five: Selective Memory. You "regroup" for living in the real world without your loved one. Yet at times something will happen. You will see someone you haven't seen since the death, or you will come across something written by the deceased or a special possession or a picture of the deceased, etc. For a few hours, a day or two, you are "down," morose and preoccupied. You seem to go through it all again. This is a short-lived condition and you go back to a more even emotional outlook.

Stage Six: Recovery. You discover a new purpose in life and begin to recommit yourself to causes and individuals in the real world. You have done with grief work. You incorporate all that is creative about your loved one into your own way of life, but hope and joy in living return. You start "to live again," to use Catherine Marshall's phrase. You begin a new chapter in your own life.

The time span in this process varies in terms of the depth and quality of your relationship to the deceased, the kind of death he or she suffered, and the degree of willingness you have to do—and insist upon yourself doing—the grief work. Your own habitual ways of handling crises of any kind have much to do with how long you are in the process.

However, as an outside time limit, let us say that if by the end of the second anniversary of the day of your loss you are still stuck in one of the first four or five of the stages, you have cause to seek professional help from your pastor, your physician, or someone they may recommend. Your basic health is at risk. You need not forever be in bondage to your grief. Life has yet much to offer you.

GRIEF AND YOUR LIFE-SUPPORT SYSTEM

The Scripture teaches you and your friends and relatives to "bear one another's burdens and so fulfil the law of Christ" (Gal. 6:2). The law of Christ is the love of his people one for another. We are to love one another as Christ loved us and gave himself for us. In your

particular grief, one of the ways of staying well is to form
and maintain an effective life-support group with whom
you share *more* than *your* grief. You do share your grief
with them, and debrief particular intense experiences
that threaten to bowl you over. However, that is not *all*
you talk about. That is not *all* you do. You listen to *their*
griefs as well. You celebrate positive and happy events
with them, also. In fact, it may take more personal
strength of character to celebrate with someone than to
commiserate with that person. If you have an effective
life-support system, you and they can both commiserate
and celebrate.

Take inventory, then, and see *if* you have such a
life-support system. Who are the persons that make up
the system? How often do you converse with them? What
do you and they talk about? Or is it that you have only *one*
person upon whom you rely, whom you trust? Are you
considerate of that one person's other responsibilities?
Or do you dominate his or her life with your demands for
time, attention, and affection? One way of staying well in
your time of grieving is to be as considerate of those near
you as you would want them to be of you. Everybody who
has reached maturity has as much need of you as you
have of them. One way of measuring your emotional
health in your grieving is to ask: Are you overdependent
on *one* person as a comforter? and, How intact is your
capacity for empathy with those who seek to comfort you?

Grief as a Power Loss

Look at your world of relationships to other persons as
a system of personal power that people in the sphere use
to *control* each other. Think of a mother and father as
controlling each other and their children. Think of the
death of one member as an event over which no one at the

time had control—that is, no one could cause it *not* to happen. Grief, then, includes a loss of power, a loss of control. You berate yourself for not being more powerful. This helplessness is something you are new at feeling. Up to the time of the death, you had the situation in hand, you were in control. Now, your grief itself becomes a means of controlling those members of your family who are left.

Usually, this kind of reaction in the grief process is found in parents of grown sons and daughters. Most commonly, the remaining parent is mourning a deceased wife or husband. It is only natural, then, to regress to an earlier state when the parent was in complete control of the sons and daughters when they were very young. Grieving over the death of a member of the family *long past the time when you should have begun to live again* becomes a means of controlling the lives of those who remain. It keeps you in power. You become a "wailing widow (or widower)." You are lonely; you complain of fears of being alone. Yet your constant rehearsal of your grief drives people who could be companionable away from you.

This is a neurotic process that calls for therapy. If you will reserve your negative conversation for an hour or two a week of counseling with a wise and patient counselor, you will make the first strong step forward breaking out of the vicious circle I have just described. You have a right to be free from such a self-defeating way of life. You have the right to reinvest your devotions to the future and to live again.

GRIEF AND DEPRESSION

The time may be three, six, twelve months, or even years since your loved one died. One day you find yourself unexplainably sad. You cannot sleep enough to meet your day's need. You have crying spells and they are uncontrollable. Your appetites for food, recreation, and sexual relations have shut down on you. You begin to feel that life is no longer a joy and may be too much for you. In brief, you are depressed. "What has this got to do with grief?" you ask.

You may have been the person at the time of the death upon whose shoulders fell the whole load of responsibility for the business details, the emotional support of the rest of the mourners. You "held up"; you did not take time to let your own feelings loose; you were the one upon whom everyone else leaned. Besides that, you just are not the type to be very emotional about things, you think. But now, sometime later, you are depressed. Your delayed grief is catching up with you. It is time for you to face it, deal with it, and work through it.

Or perhaps the death of your loved one was totally unexpected. You may have moved through all the stages of shock, numbness, and fantasy that this is not really so. Now you are overwhelmed with depression. By nature and temperament you may have gone through episodes of depression before. Now this is another one with a different cause. You cannot pull yourself out of this one.

Whatever the causes of your depression, you may be sure of this: depression can be treated with more success than you think. If it goes untreated, it can be damaging to your whole way of life. A therapist of your choosing will help you to relive your bereavement and get a fresh perspective on it. There is a range of medications to correct your sleep disorder, to stabilize the biochemical balance of your nervous system, and to elevate your mood. Then, beginning with these new strengths, he or she will collaborate with you as you rebuild your life for the long pull of the years ahead.

BIZARRE THOUGHTS AND ACTIONS

The chances are that what I will say here applies more to someone you know than to you. Some people become psychotic with a bereavement as a precipitating, though not a causal, factor. They demonstrate bizarre, hard-to-imagine thoughts and behaviors. One man, on the night that his son was killed in an auto accident, asked the resident and chaplain in the emergency room if his son's body could be stuffed by a taxidermist so that he could keep the body in his home. He was told that this is not possible and that he was trying to do something that would be damaging to himself and other family members. He then proceeded to have his son's body embalmed and placed in a sealed casket. Instead of having the body buried, he placed it in a room in his home. He built an altar there and asked visitors to worship with him.

You immediately say: "I never heard of such a thing! That's out of this world!" You readily see how bizarre it is. However, do not fear that this kind of bizarre grief reaction is going to happen to great numbers of people. Neither should you think that the tragic death "caused" this unusual reaction. When we got a previous life history of the man, we discovered other bizarre episodes in his life, none of which were prompted by a grief situation. He had already been chronically mentally ill for a long time. Yet you can see that such patients nevertheless are grieved for their loved ones even as you and I are.

Psychiatric care is needed for such florid psychotic conditions. Especially is this true if the condition has destroyed the person's capacity to function—i.e., to sleep, eat, work, and live in a reasonable degree of peace with one's family and neighbors—and if the person has been grossly hindered for as much as a year. In other words, this is not a transitory and brief state of mind. It goes on and on unless treatment is forthcoming. Furthermore, motives and threats of either suicide or vengeance to hurt or kill other people may be present. In these instances, if the person is not willing to go into a psychiatric hospital voluntarily, then legal measures may need to be taken in order to make the commitment involuntarily. This is a severe grief in its own right. If you are the relative of such a person, you have grief on top of grief. If you are that person, you need only face this crisis to see that other people are terrified by you.

Intensification of Physical Illnesses

In your struggle to stay well in the face of your grief you may find specific bodily changes coming upon you as a result of the stress. The death of a spouse, divorce from a spouse, or the death of a child rank at the top of the scale of the most stressful events that happen to people. The multiple stressing of your life at this time may (though I hope it does not) precipitate physical disorders. Heart trouble, stomach disorders, and pain-producing disorders of other kinds are likely to be intensified. Grief, especially sudden grief, exacts its toll on the body. Yet the human body is highly intelligent in its own right. Many times it has more "sense" of its own than the person who owns it has conscious awareness and wisdom.

Therefore, confer with your physician about your habit system. Seek first how you can change your habits and thinking. Wisdom and personal discipline will be your best medicine. Do not expect a pill to take away your unhappiness and grief. It will not. If, however, you cannot sleep properly, eat properly, and work properly, then your physician's prescription will help you to function better. Stay away from medications that can be bought "over the counter" at a drugstore. They have not been tailored to fit you. They may complicate rather than facilitate your health. Prescriptions are provided only after you have been diagnosed by a physician.

Your health is important. Do not neglect it. Yet in this discussion I do not want to do much more than point to your health and urge close communication with a good physician.

YOUR SPIRITUAL WELL-BEING

Let me emphasize the importance of your filling the void of your loneliness with the companionship of the Holy Spirit. You are not alone. Be of good courage. Cultivate the presence of God. Contemplate the wisdom that we shall have no other gods before him. Your (and my) great temptation in grief is to assume that our world ended when we lost our loved one. This is not so, even though it feels that way. To be fixed and stuck in this is to worship the dead. This has been the greater idolatry throughout time. But our God is the God of the living. Worship of God alone saves us from this idolatry. As the Scripture enjoins: "Keep yourselves from idols" (I John 5:21). God has not given you a spirit of fear, but a spirit of love, power, and self-control (II Tim. 1:7).

7.

Grief: A Spiritual Struggle

Y OU WILL NOT HAVE READ THE PREVIOUS PAGES OF THIS BOOK WITH-
out having sensed a mighty struggle in yourself or in
others. The purpose of this last chapter is to portray the
basically spiritual nature of this struggle, how it is a
struggle in your relation to God and to yourself. Its
further purpose is to point to sources of power for
engaging in this struggle effectively and creatively.

THE STRUGGLE WITH POWERLESSNESS

Grief is not a test of "how much you can take it." The
test is the loss of all strength. Something has happened
over which you had *no* control. You have never been so
aware of your weakness, helplessness, and powerlessness.
Nor have you ever been less willing to admit it to yourself.
As the psalmist says: "My heart throbs, my strength fails
me; and the light of my eyes—it also has gone from me"
(Ps. 38:10). Dietrich Bonhoeffer, the German pastor put
to death by the Nazis on April 9, 1945, described this dark
time as a "deliverance into Satan's hands."

> So the Christian recognizes the cunning of
> Satan. Suddenly doubt has been sown in his
> heart, suddenly everything is uncertain, what

I do is meaningless, suddenly sins of long ago
are alive in me as though they had happened
today, and they torture and torment me,
suddenly my whole heart is full of deep sorrow
for myself, for the world, for God's powerlessness over me, suddenly my vexation with life
will lead me to terrible sin, suddenly evil desire
is wakened, and suddenly the Cross is upon
me and I tremble. This is the hour of
temptation, of darkness, of defenseless deliverance into Satan's hands. (*Creation and Fall,
and Temptation*, p. 99; Macmillan Co., 1959)

This is the kind of testing from which you pray to be
delivered, a kind of evil from which you pray for
deliverance, as Jesus taught us in the Lord's Prayer. You
ask that this cup of sorrow may pass from you.

This weakness, this helplessness, this powerlessness, is
one of the reasons you have trouble accepting, admitting,
and facing up to the death of your loved one. It keeps you
from recovering from your grief. As long as you do not
accept the harsh reality of your loss, you *feel* like you are in
control. As one man said of the death of his son: "They
tell me I must accept his death. If I do that, then he will be
dead!" What he could not accept was, not that his son was
dead, but that there was nothing *he* could do to change
that fact. To do this is to confess one's weakness,
helplessness, and powerlessness. Not to do so is to allow
grief itself to become a way of life instead of recovering
from it. Martin Luther, in his *Table Talk*, gave us the clue
to accepting our own helpless weakness when he said:

The Lord our God is a God of the humble and
perplexed hearts, who are in need, tribulation
and danger. If we were strong, we would be
proud and haughty. God shows his power in
our weakness; he will not quench the glim-

mering flax, neither will he break in pieces the
bruised reed. (*The Table Talk of Martin Luther,*
edited by Thomas S. Kepler, p. 285; World
Publishing Co., 1952)

The apostle Paul described it this way:

God keeps faith, and he will not allow you to be
tested above your powers, but when the test
comes he will at the same time provide a way
out, by enabling you to sustain it. (I Cor. 10:13,
NEB)

THE SEARCH FOR MEANING

In the depths of your grief you may have been struck
by the absurdity, pointlessness, and meaninglessness of
the death of your beloved. Now, without that person, you
feel abandoned. Sometimes you even feel angry toward
him or her for dying and leaving you. You search the
inscrutable face of life as it is without that loved one. You
ask: "Is there any meaning at all to this death, and—now
that a loved one is gone—to my life from here on?"
Without some meaning, life for you either stands still or
erupts into chaos in your mind. Your persistent cry of
"Why?" concentrates this appeal for meaning.

You will search in vain for some "reason" that makes
the death of your beloved seem fair, just, and under-
standable. However, God works *after the fact* of the death
to bring meaning to your life. You go about your daily
duties, but the inner unity of your life is a jumble of
meaningless pieces. Let me tell you a parable.

When our son Bill was about five years of age, I bought
him a little balsa wood airplane. It was "powered" by a
heavy rubber band. When twisted, the rubber band
would unwind and turn the propeller. Thus the little
plane flew well outside the house where there were no

walls to hit. But one day when the weather was bad, Bill was playing in the basement with his airplane. I heard him scream with anger. I went to the basement to see what had happened to him. He had attempted to fly his plane in the basement. It had crashed into pieces as it hit the basement wall. He was crying loudly, but all of a sudden he stopped crying and began to wipe his tears and even smile.

I asked him what had happened in his mind. He said: "I know what I will do; I will take that rubber band and make me a slingshot out of it!"

Bill is thirty-three now. He has served two tours of duty in Vietnam. He has seen the pieces, not only of real airplanes, but also of human lives. He himself has experienced pain and grief. Yet this story is a parable of his life. He has a way of grieving appropriately for a while. Then he sets about perceiving a new design, a new pattern, a new use of the pieces.

Reorganizing the pieces of your life into a useful and even humorous whole calls for a pattern to go by, a design that amounts to a fresh sense of calling and vocation in dialogue with God. The meaning will not be found in explaining how God could let someone die. The meaning will lie in those spiritual discoveries of your own calling and vocation which would not likely have happened if your loss had not punctured your superficiality. You are being pushed to the depths of human life. These depths become your deceased loved one's legacy for your own survival and hope.

Your Calling and Recommitment to Life

One thing that hinders your recovery from grief is that *for you* death has no place at all in the created order of the universe. If you are like most people, death is alien to your universe, is something foreign to you. Intellectually you may admit that death happens to other people but emotionally you assume that it will never come near to you and your loved ones. The undercurrent of illusion that you are an exception and should be treated as such prevents you from devoting yourself to anything but an internal argument against death's intrusion into your personal world. Hence, you are tempted to make a vocation of grief, a work to which you devote full time. May God prevent you from this dead end of human existence. You have not been called to such a vocation. You "take your share of suffering for the sake of the Gospel, in the strength that comes from God . . . who brought us salvation and called us to a dedicated life . . . in Christ Jesus. . . . For he has broken the power of death and brought life and immortality to light through the Gospel" (II Tim. 1:8-10, NEB).

God comforts you and me with a purpose. God equips us through our suffering to *be* a comfort to other people who are grieved. As the apostle Paul states it:

> Blessed be the God and Father of our Lord Jesus Christ, the Father of mercies and God of all comfort, who comforts us in all our affliction, so that we may be able to comfort those who are in any affliction, with the comfort with which we ourselves are comforted by God. (II Cor. 1:3-4)

In brief, God saves us from self-centeredness and a "pity me" way of life by intensifying our awareness of our capacity to comfort other people in their suffering. You can visualize people you know who have been very helpful to you in your grief. You probably know them well enough to be aware that they themselves have had more grief than any ten people usually have. Yet they have a serenity, a quiet presence, and a healing kind of wisdom. They speak with you as veterans of grief. Your calling is to become somewhat that way yourself—a healer of broken hearts. What shape that calling takes will be determined by your unique personality and talents. Your particular grief enhances your unique gifts as a caring person.

The exercise of your calling, enabled by the power of the Spirit, takes you out of self-centeredness. It recenters your affections and loyalty. It is no act of disloyalty to your deceased loved one to begin to recommit your time, energy, and affection to new causes and new people. You may even find your perspective returning in such clarity that you can laugh. The memory of your loved one begins to turn up humorous and joyous things he or she said and did. You can—with some degree of forbearance—begin to see his or her faults and no longer hold on to an unbelievable kind of gilded saint. You may even begin to permit yourself to enjoy the freedom from responsibilities that the deceased's presence before death laid upon you. You begin to breathe more deeply. Your face ceases to be drawn and tense. You have, by God's grace, begun to live again.

LINCOLN CHRISTIAN COLLEGE

DATE DUE

MAR 29 '90